EBONY RHYTHM

An Anthology of Contemporary Negro Verse

EDITED BY

BEATRICE M. MURPHY

Granger Poetry Library

GRANGER BOOK CO., INC.
Great Neck, N.Y.

First Published   1948

Reprinted   1982

ISBN 0-89609-233-X

PREFACE

An anthology, in our opinion, is something like a bowl of mixed chocolates: dig into them and you can find almost any kind which suits your fancy. So, in the present volume, any lover of poetry ought to find something to suit his taste. No attempt has been made to channel the thinking of the writers, nor to confine the book to any one type of writing. We have attempted only to select what appeared to be the best of that submitted, regardless of subject matter. The only taboos were poetry containing derogatory designations—no matter how justified the occasion might seem—and the obviously risque, as not fitting to the dignity of the book.

There is bound to be comparison between this volume and *Negro Voices,* which we edited a few years ago. A critic at that time made the observation that she was disappointed because the work of the Negro poets was not dissimilar to that of any other race. We have never understood exactly what she meant, but interpreting what we believe she meant— that somehow anything a Negro does must be different simply because it was done by a Negro—we are sure some will be just as disappointed here. The Negro poets write, as poets have since they first began, about love, nature, and everyday events in the world they live in— which is an American, not a Negro, world. There is no subserviency, no stereotypes. But, putting the two volumes side by side, we believe that in the present instance the poet has grown in world outlook, and his work reflects more, and deeper, social consciousness.

Right here we would like to make the observation that editors would do the young Negro writer a greater service by demanding of him what they would demand from any other writer, rather than being swayed, by sentimental considerations of race, to "encourage" what sometimes turns out to be mediocrity rather than genius.

The editor lays no claim to profundity. Our aim has been to present a group of Negro poets, for your interest and entertainment, and for whatever benefits they may derive from the presentation.

We call special attention to the biographies because we feel they are highly significant.

BEATRICE M. MURPHY

July 1947

CONTENTS

EBONY
RHYTHM

Alice D. Anderson

The mother of six grown children, Mrs. Anderson has been writing since childhood. Her poems have been read before church and civic groups, one of them set to music by Mme. Lillian Evanti, under the title of "Himno Pan-Americano." She is at present working on a book, *Treasured Thoughts for Expectant Mothers*.

THE POET

She sees the little things that you'd pass by,
The modest violets, the mossy stones.
She hears the noises that you would not hear,
The cricket chirp, the buzz of humming bees;
She finds joy in a ray of bright sunshine,
In the first appearing of spring flowers,
In the first robin red breast's cheerful song,
In the gleaming rain drops of April's showers.

She thrills, too, at sunrises and sunsets,
And the brilliance of twilight symphonies
Stills her, a rhapsody of varied hues
All framed with myriads of cool blue stars,
A gorgeous picture in the firmament.
She sees the moon mists on the quiet stream,
God's glorified! She feels His presence near,
He walks and talks with her; love reigns supreme.

Edna L. Anderson

Edna L. Anderson is the author of *Through the Ages*, a book of verse. Her poetry has appeared in *The Crisis, New Vistas, Negro Story*, and other magazines.

IT SEEMS TO ME

Nothing's too high to reach for,
Slim though the chance may be.

A Negro can't live if a Negro can't hope—
That's the way it seems to me.

Now I'm no philosopher;
I don't have time for such.
Maybe I just got common sense
With a philosopher's touch.

So, my friend, I says to you,
"Be it, or it not be,
A Negro can't live if a Negro can't hope—
That's the way it seems to me."

Walter G. Arnold

A student at the University of Pennsylvania, Mr. Arnold,
son of a Methodist minister. and former Sergeant Major in
World War II, recently published his first book of poems,
In Quest of Gold. His objective is to "be a teacher of English
composition with writing poetry and novels as a hobby."

ENTREATY

Thou Who gave Homer for his lack of sight
A gift of song such as no other knew,
Who gave Beethoven, who was deaf, the might
To write great music, as none else can do,
O great Creator Who throughout the years
Has compensated those who were in need,
Hear me, as now I come to Thee in tears,
And to this humble prayer of mine, give heed!

Grant me, O God, for all the things that I
Will never know except as dreams, because
Thou made me black, the sight to see just why
It must be thus. Then, this dull pain that gnaws
My heart, because of all I am denied,
At last will cease; and I'll be satisfied.

INTERROGATION.

Why must a man who loves his country well,
Who has for her an honest reverence,
Who stands without a qualm, ready to sell
His dear life's blood for her continuance,
Who puts in her all his implicit trust,
Then asks no more of her for loyalty
Than that she treat him not as worthless dust
But like a man in a democracy . . .

Why must a man with all these qualities,
The kind of traits which everyone must prize,
Who's hailed by other nationalities
For his true worth, be in his nation's eyes
Seen always as a loyal colored man,
And never as a true American?

Katharine Beverly

Katharine Beverly has worked as librarian, teacher, secretary, and newspaper proof-reader, and travelled extensively in Europe, the West Indies, Mexico and Cuba. She has, since her appearance in *Negro Voices,* contributed to several anthologies, and appeared in a number of recitals, including one in London before the National Theatre Group.

NIGHT SONG

These things I hold for all the world to see:
Days strung like beads upon a silver string,
And counted hours together, short and free,
Linked by promises of a verdant Spring.
Some things I hold in silence well apart.
From untaught eyes I hold them far from view,
The silent song-beat of a lonely heart,
My arms without the feel of loving you.

I hold apart and clasp possessively
Things with your touch upon them—cry in pain
When through your window comes relentlessly
The scent of roses wet with April's rain.

DREAMS ARE SO PALE

Tuck dreams from sight in stardust; let them rest;
Lay them away in lavender, not rue.
Love-dreams can fade in too much happiness
That glows like sunlight in the heaven's blue.
Warm them with thoughts and hopes, and ever keep
Guard over dreams shut in the heart's deep tomb.
Take them not out to reminisce and weep
Over hours spent in labor from love's womb.

Dreams are so pale, so fragile, and so wan
Born of two hearts between moonmist and the dawn.

Louise Blackman

Louise Blackman is at present staff member of the Detroit
edition of the Pittsburgh *Courier*. A former WAC, she has
been writing for about 10 years, and was former City Editor
of the Michigan *Chronicle*.

RAIN WISH

You came to me this morning
Weeping in the rain . . .
My arms stretched forth to touch you
But in vain.
They clutched cold space
While aching, dreaming brain
Repeated automatically
To rhythm of the rain

O lost, O lovely love of mine,
Come back again. . . .

Come bringing light and laughter;
Leave weeping in the rain.
Come rest within these empty arms
Wherein you oft have lain.

MIRACLE

No light entered the darkened room;
Locked was the welcome door;
The farewell said . . . the gay love dead;
The vision flown forevermore.

I turned away . . . how gray the day,
How shorn of beauty . . . void of good.
O God! My eyes went heavenward,
And there You stood.

Dorothy F. Blackwell

Dorothy Blackwell holds an A.B. degree from the Louisville
Municipal College, and is now a teacher in Danville. She has
always wanted to write prose, but "verse comes easier."

ECHO

Peeved, petulant, silence tugged when
I paused there—
    at the head of the falling stair.
Step (step)
Swish (swish)
Step (step)
Swish (swish)
Sounds . . . . sounds . . . .

vibrating, scampering, spattering sounds . . . .
Sounds . . . . sounds . . . .
double-sounding echoed sounds . . . .
footsteps patting a singing song . . . .
rustlings whispering there . . . .

In the wide, deep, corridor—
    that led to the falling stair.

Peeved, petulant silence tugged . . . .
tugged when I paused there —
    at the head of the falling stair.

NOCTURNE

Dark night
And pale moonlight
Embraced
   Like
A yellow girl
And a dark
   Lover.

CRESCENDO

My blood sang to the
music of a pulsing heart
when you came near me.

Our eyes whispered moist
messages that others could not see,
when you caressed me.

Our bodies throbbed
in screaming unison
when you kissed me.

—6—

Our souls shouted prayers
of thanksgiving
when you embraced me.

Samuel E. Boyd

Discharged from the Army in February 1946, Mr. Boyd,
after serving for two years in the South Pacific, is now employed in New York City as Social Investigator. This is his
first appearance in print except in school publications.

REBEL

They piled high stones
Around his bier
Into a monument,
And angels starred and studded it
To make his rest content;
But I surmise
That he'll soon rise
And blast his discontent;
For he is one who cannot stand
White walls and cold cement.

DANCE FINALE

I, too, shall dance the dance of death
On earthless, timeless ground;
With rhythmic beat I'll dip and sway—
Go 'round and 'round and 'round.

I, too, shall know the silences
Encumbered in the earth;
Divorced of soul, I shall lie down
Like ash upon a hearth.

I, too, shall know the answer to
The reasons why and how.
I, too, shall be, in spite of death,
A blossom on a bough.

AND SO TOMORROW....

Since losing you
I have not wept
Or cursed my lot
As lovers do
When love is lost
And not forgot.
Day is still day,
And time, articulate,
Blows taps for those who
Looking back stumble their way
Across this scale of rising crests.
Tomorrow still provokes my pride
And I must till and toil, though you be gone . . .
And memory saunters at my side.

TOMORROW'S WINDS

Tomorrow's winds will blow my brain
As clear, as calm, as cool,
As dawn upon a mountain top,
As starlight on a pool.
No more this ebbing turbulence
Of you and me and this . . .
Tomorrow's winds will blow it all
Into a mad abyss.

Arthur Braziel

Arthur Braziel, 18 years old, has never published before, but is working hard to become a successful writer.

VIRGIN FIELD

Untouched by the plow,
Free of the grain,
Innocent of the sweat of man or beast,
Bathed only in the waters of the rain,
Warmed by the sun time and time again,
Painted by the moon that shines from beyond—
You are virgin now—
But for how long?

Jean Brierre

A native of Haiti, Mr. Brierre was former Secretary of the Haitian Legation in Paris, and is in charge of the cultural section of Haitian Ministry of Foreign Affairs. He is Director and Editor of the Haitian political and literary newspaper, *Clartes*. He has published many poems in his own country.

AREYTOS
(To Violetta Maria)

Violetta,
Your beauty revives the splender of the Indian age,
Your tresses date from the fourteen hundreds.
A Spaniard loved them more than gold
And left in their dark undulations
The disconsolate impress of his loving hand.

Maria,
My dreams, like conquistadores,
Steal at times

The subtle treasures hidden in your hair.
Violetta,
The smiling plains of virgin Hispaniola beheld,
Trembling centuries ago,
The languor of your step.
And coming after you today
Among the shades of evening,
I have the strange impression
That you bifurcate the path of history
At the crossroad of the centuries.

Your skin, Maria,
Is not only an Antillean night,
Where dwell without number
The perfume of corollas and fruits—
On your skin, Maria,
My closed eyes see landscapes of an oasis
Overhung by mirage
And the dense shadow of the Sphinx.

Is your gesture Indian or Negro?
Is it the caress of fantoms
Or the loosened curves of an amphora?
And when you hold in your dark hands
The face surprised by love,
You make of it a thing of art,
A miniature from an ancient grotto,
The coloring of a drum,
In the manner of a masterpiece of Indian or Negro.

Dance, Violetta,
Your steps brighten the stars in the dust of the
                              shadows.
Speak, Maria,
Your teeth fill the vacant night with flowers.
Walk, Violetta,
Your silhouette lights up the black window.
Sing, Maria,

As night becomes still,
Your intimate song.

And I, impenitent poet,
An old flute that sounds when you pass,
I see with melancholy,
Among the branches entwined
With your memories and fecund thoughts—
I see with poignant fervor
Suffering in your profund eyes
The pupils of Queen Anacaona lighted with love and
poetry.

Translation by Haitian Embassy, Washington, D. C.

HARLEM

I have seen you suffer in the midst of winters,
and your shadow erect amidst the street lamps
has told me often of its hunger at the doors
    of the eating houses.
I have seen you bleed at times on the sidewalks,
and I have not heard your agony make complaint.
I have seen you adorned in the springtime,
    bedecked in laughter and joy,
    dressed in sunshine and silk,
    singing and dancing,
    singing strange songs,
the heavy songs of sirens,
    of voyaging,
    of calls and of silence on forgotten seas,
    of bitter songs,
    ending with outbursts of laughter
    like mighty cymbals.
I have seen you dancing in whirlwinds
    like the frenzied,
    celebrating some god hidden in the
    depths of you.

Where, O Harlem, do you sleep?
Perhaps you pluck the leaves of the last star
in your fragile cup
and find again at the portals of the dawn
    the trouble,
    the toil,
    the weariness,
    the poverty,
    the hour which sounds like a knell
    and your heart, weary and alone
    on the road, hostile and black.

Translated by John F. Matheus

TO PAUL ROBESON

I hear in your voice the birth of the world
From the first quivering of the light grass
To the gusts of horror that shake the deserts.
I hear your voice coming from the depth of the ages,
Laden with the first complaints
And the first sorrows of the black man.
The first staff on which
He transcribed his sorrow—
I divine in your voice
That he traced in on the glebe
In the ardent colors of blood and of the sun.

One day,
Leaving his shadowy cavern
After shaking off the oppression of centuries and of
                    races,
Still bruised with chains,
Panting
From having held on his shoulders and in his wounded
                    hands
The joys of the world,
The opulence of the world,
—12—

The Negro, finding life anew,
Will transform the knell of his heart into eternal
carillons.

Then from all these past sorrows,
From all these Calvaries,
From all these laments without echo,
You will make a sounding orchestra,
With the sun and the moon
For cymbals,
And dominating the chorus of all anguish,
Your voice,
Profound as the night,
Vast like the deserts,
Immense like the route of centuries,
Will sing to the subdued echo
The sacred hymn of black Redemption.
Translation by Haitian Embassy, Washington, D. C.

Iola M. Brister

Iola M. Brister was the first Negro student in the Los
Angeles City College Drama Department. She was a charter
member of the New Negro Theatre, and played an important
role in Langston Hughes' play, "Don't You Want to Be
Free?" A fashion designer, she turns out California leisure
wear accessories under the tag of "Iola of Hollywood." She
has also appeared in print with stories, plays and articles. Her
poetry in *Negro Voices* was widely acclaimed.

EPIGRAM

Were I not black
You would not turn
And stare at me
Here in the concert hall.
For in all else—

The clothes,
The smugness,
The feigned half-smile—
I am, too, like you.

A NEGRO SPEAKS OF NIGHT

Although I work and sweat
And gleam so shiny bright
In noon-day sun,
I have known wondrous nights.

I have known night
Along the Nile
All stars
And moon.
Pale silver light
Filtering through
The silhouette of trees.

I have known night
Down on the delta,
All warm
And humid
While soothing
Insect songs
Lulled my south to sleep.

I have known night
Along the "Avenue"
All joy
And heady laughter
And throbbing songs
Among shadows
And glaring city lights.

I have known wondrous nights . . . .

Delores A. Brown

Delores Aramenta Brown, a graduate of Virginia Union University, is at present teacher of English at the R. R. Moton High School in Farmville, Va.

UPON LOOKING AT LOVE

Like a wild flame it leaps
And speaks to the innermost
Portion of the soul.
It knows no master and chooses not one;
Cannot be touched and yet its force is
Stronger than a thousand magnets.
As beautiful as a golden sunset,
As strange as the whistle of the wind,
Gentle as the purr of a kitten—
But alas! how cruel love can be
To some of its victims!

Joe C. Brown

A native of Mississippi, Mr. Brown, who now makes his home in Chicago, has been writing poetry since his high school days and his work has appeared in *People's Voice,* Jackson (Miss.) *Advocate,* and other papers. Still in his thirties, he is the father of six children—four daughters and two sons.

SIGNS OF SLEEP

Fear not the dog's howl.
Be not moved by the screeching owl.
Cover not the mirror to hide my face,
Nor stop the clock's hourly pace.
Let not my loved ones weep
When that mystic hour comes for me
To sleep.

RUSTIC LOVE

Love is strong
As the scent of onions,
Tender as the shoots of cabbage sprouts;
Sweet like the taste of voodoo sorghum . . .
And muddy as branch water.

George B. Browne

George Bagby Browne, a native of Washington, D. C., was
graduated from West Virginia State College in January, and
is continuing his work in the teaching field. This is his first
published work.

THE TRAIN RIDE

I took a train to be by your side
And all along the way,
Each tree, flower and field
Resembled something of you.
By the time I neared the station
I knew just how you would look, hold me,
And kiss me.

Naomi E. Buford

A former nursery school teacher, Mrs. Buford is now a
housewife in Danville, Illinois.

HERITAGE

The world is mine.
I have cattle feeding on a thousand hills;
And watersprings . . . clear, sparkling, gurgling rills
    Among the mountain passes;

My lambs within the meadows stray—
And, contented, feed the livelong day
    Upon the tender grasses.

The sea is mine.
Its blue expanse now lies at rest
While sea-gulls hover over its breast
    In act of sweet devotion.
But oft the waves dash wild and high
And the breakers roar as the sea gulls cry
    Their tribute to the ocean.
The fields are mine,
The fragrant woodland flowers,
The singing birds, the butterflies and bees
The twining bowers
And the fishes of the sea.
I am a queen upon the universe:
All these belong to me.

The world is mine.
I have cattle feeding on a thousand hills;
And watersprings . . . clear, sparkling, gurgling rills
    Among the mountain passes;
My lambs within the meadows stray
And, contented, feed the livelong day
    Upon the tender grasses.

Frederica Katheryne Bunton

Frederica K. Bunton is an honor graduate from the University of Dayton where she served as Associate Editor of the school paper. She works in the Dayton Public Library, and is doing graduate work at the University.

YOU TAUGHT ME LOVE

You taught me love
And then I ceased to know

That love must have its aftermath,
Its galling, bitter afterglow.
Ah, yes, you taught me love.

You taught me love
And then I learned too late
That love when scorned begets pure hate,
Ah, bitter, bitter fate
When first you taught me love.

You taught me love
And then I felt disdain
That too much sun must end in rain
And love too deep brings only pain.
Ah, yes, you taught me love.

You taught me love
And then was born that strife,
The fire with which my soul is rife.
Ah, love, ah, light, you took my life
When first you taught me love.

John W. Burton

Mr. Burton, a native of Washington, D. C., is a teacher in the D. C. Junior High Schools. He served as a member of the Editorial Board for *Negro Voices*. His poetry has appeared in several anthologies, including *Negro Voices*, in newspapers, and in the *Bronxville Villager* and *Pulse* magazines.

BLACK CAMEO ON PINK QUARTZ

Yours is not a beauty
To go unobserved
By others, nor myself,
But one to haunt

Our waking, sleeping, living,
And maybe our dying hours.
Yours is a beauty
Of dignity and of grace;
Yours is a beauty
Of line and of strength
Rivalled only by
The forest's richest ebony;
A beauty
Startlingly clothed in rose.

VIGNETTE

I

You took it all so casually—
Like the wearing of an old house frock—
Until it has frightened me
To know that I
So unwittingly
Played the part of a fool
Who thoughtlessly lives
His moment to the full.

Now I am full of regret;
While you are quick to forget.

II

As if on a hurried errand
Two planets run their course
Before a pursuant moon
That leaves no clouds
To hinder its chase
Across the betwinkled sky
Of an October midnight.

Yesterday
I returned to an old, old haunt
Where we spent moments
Glorious and many.
Before
The place was alive and real
But yesterday
It was filled with cobwebs.

PRIDE

Martyrdom
Is not our course
Cry my heart
And soul aloud.
Yet for some reason
I have chosen now
To be proud.

Alpheus Butler

Alpheus Butler has had poetry published in more than 25 volumes of poetry. He is the Editor of *The Parnassian* and *The Twentieth Century Review*, both periodicals published by the Laurel Publishers; author of *Quests with Pegasus, Primrose and Thistle* and *Sepia Vistas;* is a graduate of the University of Denver.

PRIMROSE AND THISTLE

I always sought to fill the days I knew
With many hours of goodness, truth, and mirth.
I sought to find the better, finer view
Of earth and life and folk. I knew the worth

Of ideals. When my searching, questing soul
Encountered dark, deep, nether minds designed
To crush a heart immaculate and whole,
I sought new fields to leave those minds behind.

And so I found a primrose by the road
Of Life. Nearby there grew the thistle weed.
Both were within an open air abode
And strived to live. The thistle was the seed
Of discord, but the primrose flower won
The final right to thrive beneath the sun.

MAID AND VIOLINIST

I am a rover ever wandering far
Into the hidden places of a soul.
I am a crooner singing to a star
And yearning for all things that make life whole.
I love a maiden in a chenille gown:
The touch of her warm hand, her velvet hue.
My silvered hair is like a gleaming crown.
Her lips are rubies mellow, lush and true.

I play my violin, wailing melodies
So plaintive, pure, so filled with notes of joy.
I tell my maiden I will strive to please
Her whims, her fancies. She is very coy
When, dreamily, I trill a fragile tune.
Each note is just a lovely, tender croon.

PORTRAIT OF A POET

I learned while in my teens of notes, of chords,
Of music blithe and sombre, gay and sad.
I learned to know the deeper, wiser words
Of masters of the art of thought. How glad

I always was when dawn or evening came
And prayers were said. I liked the holy creeds
We learned to chant. My heart was like a flame
Burning with passion for immortal deeds.

And when I sought with parchment, ink and quill
To fashion worlds nearer my heart's desire
Than this I knew, I sought the tallest hill
And stood there searching for celestial fire.
I found the muse of song, Melpomene,
And vintages of rarest melody.

Hood C. Butler

Hood C. Butler was born in the Philippine Islands of American parentage. He served in Liberia in World War II. Some
of his work appeared in *The Anthology of College Poetry*
sponsored by the National Poetry Association.

EBONY RHYTHM

From the land of Afric palm and desert sand
Came rhythm, ebony rhythm,
A sleeping giant unawakened.
Dormant in the breast of man,
Springing from its Afric womb,
Nurtured in the tropic sun,
Ebony rhythm in the moonlight
Danced to savage throbbing drums.
With bodies lithe, and skins like satin,
They danced with pagan delight,
Sons and daughters of the jungle,
Ebony rhythm in the night.

David Wadsworth Cannon, Jr.

David Wadsworth Cannon, Jr., a graduate of Hillsdale College, was nominated as its Rhodes Scholar from Michigan. He received the M.A. degree from the University of Michigan in 1932. While teaching for four years at Virginia State College, he made two concert tours with a student verse-speaking choir which he sponsored, and then entered Columbia University to study for his doctorate, his graduate study being made possible by his election as a Fellow of the National Council on Religion in Higher Education in 1936, and a Rosenwald Fellowship in 1937. While at Columbia, he was stricken with a cerebral hemorrhage and died. The poems printed herein are from a volume of his work collected by his mother, Mrs. Gertrude Cannon Morris, and published by the National Council on Religion in Higher Education.

M O U N T A I N S

The weight of mountains is upon me.
Tall stretching pines, pregnant with cone, yawn with
    the swaying bodies of their unborn kind.
Only the west wind understood.
Full well he knew their backs would bend with
    cushioned cloud weight earthward.
That they would only know the same dark valleys
    that their forebears knew.

Yet he was free to roam—
To sense the ecstasy of life . . .
And never feel the pallid hand of Death.

Peaks pinch soft clouds!
And they—young virgins of a wind-swept day—did
    weep and knew not why.
Flowers caught their tears—
    Such wet pain is the meat of flowered laughter.

Snows hugged bold young summits.
Old spinsters!

Vainly snatching love from youth lest they should die
    ere they knew life—
A frozen, sterile union,
Which countless dawns and fervid twilights have not
    kindled into birth.

Pine, heavy with cone!
Peaks, cloud burdened!
Summits, snow weary!
The weight of mountains is upon me.

BOSTON TEA

"The ladies of the D.A.R.
Meet here today at four, for tea."
Malinda Attucks washed the plates,
And baked small cakes for thirty-three.

She smiled; and looked at Crispus Attucks,
"Black Martyr—Independence War,"
Who mused in marble silence on the square . . .
Then, she served tea to thirty-four.

TO NITA

You—
You are a forest, cool, lush, and green,
And I—
Only a little bird, lost in the arms of your smallest
                    tree.
You—
You are a quaint old garden in springtime,
And I—
Only a bumblebee
Caught in a spider's web

Spun in your shyest flower.
You—
You are the sea at moonrise,
Placid—deep . . .
And I
Only a silver fish fashioning a ripple—close,
Close near the heart of you.

WORLD WEARINESS

I have grown weary of this carnal bark,
Of red-tufted heart that drums a hollow bough.
The Lonely One was nailed upon a tree.
In every vein I am as bruised now.
And yet, no storm can wash me out to sea.
My dying roots eke deeper than the earth.
Like Nicodemus, old and facing death,
They seek again the source of second birth.

When autumn came, the frightened birds obeyed.
I was alone, and knew no song to sing.
And though this winter's fury whips me bare,
I know that I shall leaf another spring.

For I was living when this puny world
Leaped full-grown from the forehead of the sun.
I struggled through archean ooze and climbed
Upon the land, and I became as one
With all the silent crust-bound creeping things.

Then, weary of the earth, I wooed the sky . . .
And now again I seek the soft brown loam.
For though a hundred million years are spent,
I still remember nights when silver foam
From moon-drenched lakes was frothing at my feet.

I have grown weary of this carnal bark;
I sense the pulse of aeons yet to be.
Push out strong rootlets, light-bound prisoned soul,
And wind yourself around infinity.

DARK LOVE

Dark laughter, like new sparkling wine,
Will sour when bottled up too long.
Dark lips, like black dew-sweet cherries,
Will crack unless they frame a song.

Dark hands, like sable willow trees,
Will droop when withered by the sun.
Dark feet, like cats before a fire,
Will rest when winter's day is done.

Dark eyes, like purple tulip cups,
Will close when flushed with hot wet pain.
Dark love, like footprints in white snow,
Will melt when riddled by cold rain.

INSIGHT

If I could ever know
The loneliness of silent falling star,

Or break the fragile bands
That Saturn wears apart, with magic rod,

Or ever ever thread
The endless maze of starbright milky way,

Then I could comprehend the Great Gestalt
And soar from man to God.

Howard Carpenter

Howard Carpenter joined the Navy in 1945 and is now stationed in California. This is his first published work.

SOLAR FLIGHT

To touch! To burn my palm,
To send a pain into my mind
And fire a flame within my heart—

To touch you would send me past
All earthly bounds—
To bring back the milky way,
To soothe my burning palm.

Herman J. D. Carter

Herman J. D. Carter sold his first story in 1931. Since then he has published poetry and prose regularly, worked for a while in radio, served as correspondent for the Associated Negro Press, the Scott Newspaper Syndicate, the Pittsburgh *Courier,* and the Afro-American newspapers. He founded *The American Negro Mind* Magazine and the "First Novel Syndicate," both of which were suspended when the author entered World War II. He is the author of *The Scottsboro Blues,* a booklet of verse, and has appeared in numerous anthologies. He is at present employed by the Federal Government in Washington, D. C., and seeking publishers for a book of poetry, a novel, and several other manuscripts.

THE VOICE OF THE HILL

"Hark!
Stranger, rest your weary self. . . .
The voice you hear
Is the voice of the hill. . . .
I am the first born of my kind. . . .

I suffered in the twirl of flaming disaster. . . .
And shrank with the passing of centuries. . . .
I've kissed the ceiling of the Universe
With my lips pallid and white . . .
In my bosom rest the bones of men;
In my dimples soldiers have slept,
Groaned and died;
In my wrinkles, blood. . . .
Like liquid fire has flowed . . . . . .

"I am the hill,
The mighty hill
Who birthed the Rock of Ages."

A POETESS
(To E. D. D.)

Rapidly
She jots her thoughts
Given
From
The gods. . . .

Then
Paints them
With knowledge
From
On High. . . .

And
Boils them
Till they're small
Like
Desert sands. . . . . .

MOUNTAIN IN A STORM

The sky is angry,
It brandishes fiery swords
Portraying
The nakedness of the valley,
And gaunt winding roads,
Bathed with angels' tears. . . .
Fading into infinity.
The tall pines reach for heaven,
Then bow their heads in prayer,
As the wilderness cries out for mercy.

NEGRO AUDIENCE

Splotches from the paint brush of the heavenly artist,
God,
Fell over the faces of Humanity. . . .
Making them a thousand shades. . . .

How beautiful is such a panorama!

Nell Chapman

Nell Clayton Chapman is a dressmaker in Massillon, Ohio.
Member of the Board of Trustees of her local Urban League,
she has written several short stories, plays, a book of poetry,
and is now working on a novel.

BREAD ON THE WATER

Bread, cast on the water, will return . . .
That's enough to live by.
Debts of life are paid
In full and like proportion

According to the texture of the stuff
From which the loaf is made. . . . .

Hungry dogs ate wicked Jezebel
Outside the frowning walls of old Jezreel,
And there were none to mourn her,
None to feel

The dagger thrust of parting's pain.
There was no weeping there,
And, if one agonizing prayer
Rose to Heaven's gate,
It rose impotent; and too late,
And crashed to earth again.

REQUIEM
(*In memory of Franklin Delano Roosevelt*)

The world had steeled itself for death that day;
Anguish was an old, familiar fright.
It was not strange to see
Eyes dulled by misery,
Or hear of one more heart that broke
Beneath the crushing yoke
Of gathered tears.
Death was no alien thing,
For those were desperate and trying years.

But we had not become inured to pain . . .
As if to test the measure of our strength,
Across the shuddering earth, there came, at length,
A tense, hushed message,
Stammering a name.
"We interrupt—we interrupt," it said,
"The world must know,
The President—is dead."

We heard, and stood in awe, and unbelief,
He, who, with matchless fellow-feeling
Bore a troubled nation's grief,
Lay still in death.

The tired heart,
Too burdened with the common woe, and weal,
Had ceased to beat, to know, to feel
The country's sorrow.
The voice, that millions knew to say,
"My friends . . ."
To rich and poor alike,
Of it, we could no longer borrow faith.

Oh, let him lie!
If there be regions where the valiant dead
At last, may rest,
He will not lose the trail . . .
He'll find, unerringly, that haven of the blest;
For steadily, by night and day,
The blazing light of battle stars upon his breast
Will guide him on his way.

Marcus B. Christian

Marcus B. Christian was Supervisor of the Dillard University Negro History Unit of the Federal Writers' Project. In 1943 he was awarded a Rosenwald Fellowship to do further work in the history of the Negro in Louisiana. Subsequently he was appointed Assistant in the Dillard University Library, where he is now employed. His poems and articles have appeared in *The Crisis, Opportunity, Phylon, The Louisiana Weekly, Negro Voices,* etc.

DARK HERITAGE

I helped to build this great America—
Started her up from rude huts

Thrown down in the midst of wildernesses.
I beat back those wildernesses,
Dared the ever-advancing forests,
Plowed and planted,
Hoed and harvested,
To feed her weak and disheartened colonists,
Besieged by fear and Indians.

I helped to build this great America;
I watched her shore-line creep
From Maine and Massachusetts
And Tidewater Virginia
Down through the Carolinas
To the Florida Everglades.

I fought Indians, Redcoats
And the stony, barren soil of New England;
I tilled the great Virginia estates—
The homes of Presidents;
I sang in the rice-fields of Georgia and the Carolinas;
Toiled in the swamps and on the sugar and cotton
                        plantations
   of Louisiana and Mississippi,
While the bull-whip of the overseer
Zigzagged like black lightning above my head
And cracked like the thunder of doom.
As I bowed down
In tobacco-fields, rice-fields, cane-fields, corn-fields
   and cotton-fields,
I sang so sweetly
That America believed me happy.
Then, gathering about her the airs of a Democracy,
She stretched forth welcome hands
To the dispossessed millions of Europe:
The Irish, German, West End Englishman, Italian,
                        Frenchman,
Spaniard, Portuguese, Slovak, Pole, Jew and
                        Armenian, saying:
"Come unto me, all ye that labour and are heavy-
                        laden,

and I will give you rest."
But I toiled on.

I toiled on until honest men could stand the sight no
longer
Of my black back, bleeding and raw,
Bowed down in humble, earth-kissed supplication
Before the Gods of Greed.
And then, at last, contending streams of blood,
Merging, made closer this great land of ours.

I saved America from discord.
I caught the flying javelins of hate against my own
bosom,
Keeping them free of the Catholic and Protestant,
Republican and Democrat,
Irish and German,
Blond and Brunette,
Native and Alien Stock,
Pilgrim and Puritan.
The fear of me made all men cease their bickerings
And I became the scapegoat of the nation.

In times of stresses, wars and blasting storms,
This one thing I shall evermore remember:
That all of the strength and the blood and the sweat
of me—
That all of my longings, my sorrows, my hopes and
my joys
Went into making this great land of ours;
That this is my land by the right of both God and of
man—
That this is my land, wet with my own life's blood—
That it is enriched by the flesh and bones of my
fathers—
That this land is mine, grown big through my pain
and my suffering;
That all I am today and ever shall be
Lies deeply buried in her plains and valleys,

Swamps, hills and mountains,
Meadows, lakes and streams.
I shall forever be a part of her
And she will always be a part of me.

SELASSIE AT GENEVA

They could have stayed the iron hand of might
And fought for right down to the earth's last man,
But louder voices brayed into the night,
So, jackals ended what the League began.
Now suave-voiced diplomats drone on and on;
Geneva's air is rife with fear and hate,
While at the council table fights alone
The fallen ruler of a member State.
Pile lies upon wrongs, ring the curtain down
Upon the closing scene of this last act;
The King of Kings now yields his ancient crown
To those who signed the Non-Aggression Pact,
As weaker nations vanish, one by one . . .
Blow, bugles! Armageddon has begun!

"GO DOWN, MOSES!"
(Berlin, 1938)

In great Berlin, each weary night on night,
Go frightened souls who even fear to sleep,
As racial hatred rears its ugly might,
And terrors in their cloaks of darkness creep.
The while men tramp the streets with hopes all gone,
The Gods of Greed, with lashing whips of hate,
Drive maddened Nordics onward—ever on—
To slay and plunder in the name of "State."

O Moses, who, in mounting fury, killed
Proud Egypt's son who wronged the Israelite,
The spirit of the Pharaohs is not stilled,
For the first-born still dies by day and night;
So go you where crazed Aryan hate holds sway
And smite with flame the Pharaohs of today.

THE CRAFTSMAN

I ply with all the cunning of my art
This little thing, and with consummate care
I fashion it—so that when I depart,
Those who come after me shall find it fair
And beautiful. It must be free of flaws—
Pointing no laborings of weary hands;
And there must be no flouting of the laws
Of beauty—as the artist understands.
Through passion, yearnings infinite—yet dumb—
I lift you from the depths of my own mind
And gild you with my soul's white heat to plumb
The souls of future men. I leave behind
This thing that in return this solace gives:
"He who creates true beauty ever lives."

James (Nakisaki) Christopher

James (Nakisaki) Christopher was born, and still lives, in
Chicago, Illinois. Interested in sports of all kinds, he was
welterweight runner-up twice for the CYO boxing champion-
ship of Chicago.

LULLABY TO A DREAM
(To Evelyn Brookins)

As you go dreaming, save a dream for me,
A dream of gay, inconsequential things,

When all we knew was yet to be,
  And our illusions colored all our springs.
And darling, while you dream, I hope that you recall
  A moon that dipped across a lover's sky,
And the tiny inn we sought when night would fall . . .
  The candle light, the wine and you and I.

There is an end to laughter in the rain.
  There is an end to the shadowed streets we knew,
And yet, the past cries out to me again.
  It is a simple thing that I asked of you;
As you go dreaming, save a dream for me,
  Spun from the gossamer of what used to be.

Peter Wellington Clark

Peter Wellington Clark is a teacher in New Orleans; author
of *Delta Shadows,* a pictorial study of Negro life in New
Orleans; and editor of *Arrows of Gold,* an anthology of
Catholic verse. While in the Armed Forces (where he was a
Lieutenant), he compiled an anthology of creative writings
of Negro soldiers of World War II, *No Badge of Color,* now
in process of publication. Former editor of the *Xavier Alumni
Voice* (from which University he holds an M.A. degree) and
three Armed Forces publications, *Vanguard, Retort,* and
Attack.

PARADOX

How strange the fairest pearls
Are found deep in the ocean's womb,
And yet life's crowning joys abound
Beyond the vaunted tomb.

How strange the rarest flowers bloom
Above the eagle's perch,
But still the staunchest souls are those
Who relinquish not the search.

How odd the purest lilies grow
On slimy water's edge—
Yet often the bravest souls are caught
In Fortune's gruesome wedge.

How strange that light and shadows
So seldom dwell apart—
And yet the gravest scars are found
Upon the human heart!

REALITY

Tonight I push aside
My own small dream—
The one of valleys green
And sunset's soothing glow;
For now I must think
Of things to come,
Of rifle fire and battle din,
And victories which hinge
Upon a single shot or shell—
Tonight I push aside my own small hope,
The one of a house with green shutters
And violets on the lawn,
For close ahead lie
Missions grim, foreboding,
On fields aghast with smoke and flame—
And yet I know
My own small dream, my own small wish,
Cannot be realized
Until each cannon's mouth is hushed,
Until each plane is moored in hangars
Freed of bombs.
When this great task is through,
I shall reshape my dream,
For with peace I'm sure
The lawns will greener seem—
And violets sweeter bloom.

DESERTED VILLAGE

(*Reconversion* 1946
Design inspired by latest headline)

Ten thousand millhands
Are still today;
Giant factories idly stand;
No more gray smoke
From stacks shall ooze
For strikes have swept the land.

A hundred ships
Shall steam no more
For foreign harbors bound;
For decks once chock with
Cargoes rare stretch bare
As Gobi's ground.

A million wheels and dynamos
Shall generate no heat,
And power-driven robots
Stand like soldiers in defeat.

A billion tons of merchandise
Shall mold on dusty shelves,
While floors once trod
By chore-bound feet
Shall murmur to themselves.

Twelve million men
With shrunken cheeks
Shall plead, aye, beg for work—
While Industry, herself, lies stabbed
By Greed and Glutton's dirk.

Alas, blind waste has blocked
The paths which Labor trod;
And atheists now ridicule
The pauper's faith in God.

—38—

Behold! a Universe's fate
Upon a guillotine :—
One half the earth is
Rich and fat, the other—
Shrivelled, lean!

HISTORIC EPISODES

Toussaint
Sticking out his tongue
At Napoleon Bonaparte,
The iron-willed Corsican;

John Brown
Clenching determined fist
At despots, who would enslave
Their ebony brothers;

Sojourner
Slinking through the cypress swamps,
Like a spirit in disguise,
Carrying Liberty in her bosom;

Lincoln
Climbing the splintered rostrum
At Gettysburg—with a brow furrowed
By care, but lighted by courage;

Dunbar
Singing in the wilderness,
Penning lines destined to grace
The starlit scrolls of posterity;

Christ
Hanging on the Cross of Calvary
Amid the scathing shouts and jeers—
Shedding His blood for humanity!

Helen F. Clarke

Helen F. Clarke was educated at Bennett College and Atlanta University. She lives in Washington, D. C., and is employed by the Federal Government. Her main literary interest is writing and illustrating nursery rhymes for children.

SHADOWS

Did you ever watch the brilliance
Of a setting summer sun
Fade into the dusk of evening
As though now, her tasks all done,
She makes way for night and shadows;

As though the sunbeams in their glory
Seemed to realize that they
Must depart into the heavens, and
Leave the loveliness of day—
Leave it to the night and shadows?

Did you ever watch the shadows
As they played against your wall,
Silhouettes of varied contours,
Change and jump, rise and fall?

Did you ever watch the shadows
With a very little child;
Talk with him about the figures
And his fancies free and wild?

See now, there's a pixie;
You think he's going to run?
Oh, no, he's not afraid of us—
Don't move! Oh, see, he's gone!

But there's a great big bunny
Right there beside the door.
Yes, it's moving; see it, darling?
Now its head is on the floor.

Where, dear? Oh, yes, he's kneeling—
A little boy like you;
It looks as though he is saying his prayers;
Soon that's what you must do.

Yes, the shadows will remain here
After you have gone to bed,
And some will play about your pillow;
Some will dance around your head.

No, you'll not see them on waking,
For at first signs of the day,
Together with the night and darkness
All the shadows steal away.

It is fun to watch the shadows.
Let us watch them every night
Before the evening sunset
Gives way to fainter light.

Did you ever watch the shadows
As they played against your wall
Silhouettes of varied contours,
Change and jump, rise and fall?

YOU ARE BLACK

When the ladder to success is broken
They all tell you, "Use the stairs."
But just you try ascend that staircase—
They'll inform you that it's theirs.
Even ask 'em for an old one
Out of use and in the back,
Hear them answer,
"You'll get nothing.
Don'tcha know, boy, you are black?"

John Henrik Clarke

John Henrik Clarke studied creative writing at various intervals over a period of seven years. One of his short stories was included in O'Brien's *Best American Short Stories of 1940*. He served as a Master Sergeant in World War II. His work has appeared in the *Crisis, Poet Lore, New Horizons, Opportunity, Negro Story*, Chicago *Defender*, Pittsburgh *Courier, People's Advocate,* and other periodicals. His first book of poetry, *Rebellion in Rhyme,* will be published soon.

"SING ME A NEW SONG"

Sing me a new song, young black singer,
Sing me a song with some thunder in it,
And a challenge that will
Drive fear into the hearts of those people
Who think that God has given them
The right to call you their slave.
Sing me a song of strong men growing stronger
And bold youth facing the sun and marching.
Sing me a song of an angry sharecropper
Who is not satisfied with his meager share
Of the products that he squeezed from the earth
While watering the earth with his sweat and tears.
Sing me a song of two hundred million Africans,
Reviving the spirit of Chaka, Moshesk and Menelik,
And shouting to the world:
"This is my land and I shall be free upon it!"
Put some reason in my song and some madness, too.

Let the reasons be the kind of reason
Frederick Douglas had
When he was fighting against slavery in America.
Let the madness be the kind of madness
Henri Christophe had when
He was driving Napoleon's army from Haitian soil.

Sing me a song with some hunger in it, and a
              challenge, too.
Let the hunger be the kind of hunger
Nat Turner and Denmark Vesey knew,
When they rose from bondage and inspired
Ten thousand black hands to reach for freedom.

Let the challenge be the kind of challenge
Crispus Attucks made
While dying for American Independence.

Don't put "I ain't gonna study war no more" in my
              song.
Sing me a song of a people hungry for freedom
Who will study war until they are free!

INQUIRY

How can you sing, America,
With your souls baptized in glee,
Advertising your greatness,
Boasting of your victories,
While men denied justice
Are hanging from your trees?

MEDITATIONS OF A
EUROPEAN FARMER

Where now shall I lay my head?
The fields which once yielded me
Both shelter and bread
Are now odored with rotting dead.
Since that horde of strangers
Trampled upon my land,
Planting both dead flesh and lead.
I wonder, will the fields ever again
Yield edible bread.

AMERICA

I love this arrogant young nation
Who parades her glory
Like a saucy maiden in a new dress. . . .
I am warmed by its bigness
And strengthened by its zest.
In spite of its shortcomings
And its overrated might,
I will not yield one inch of it
Without a sturdy fight.

NO TEARS

Shed no tears for the strong nations
Now crumbling . . .
Shout gleefully as they fall!
The next great glory will belong to the people
Who have lived so long
Without any glory at all.

BOMBARDMENT AND AFTERMATH

The night passed over
And the day was born
Amid the rumble of man's eternal wrong . . .
This tragedy dwarfed every smile,
Silenced every song;
There was nothing but scattered pity
In this grotesque place
That once was a city.

Mary Wilkerson Cleaves

Mary Wilkerson Cleaves graduated *cum laude* from Tougaloo (Miss.) College, and taught for a while in a Mississippi high school, where she sponsored a student publication. At present, a bride of a few months, she resides in California and is a student of radio writing, but her main literary interest is writing poetry.

BLACK SOLDIER

I look into the eyes of one returning
　From distant lands.
Over his shoulder the duffle bag, souvenirs
　In his hands.

Outwardly, his face, his whole appearance
　Is just the same.
Deep in his eyes I see the horror he has seen
　And feel the pain

Which he has felt, fighting a battle
　So hardly won
Before again is heard the battle cry for
　Others just begun.

For he is black: for him the victor's song
　Does not mean cease;
And all his kind must harder fight
　To win their peace.

For him still stands the specter of
　A rope-decked Tree;
For him still waits the menial job—
　To bend the knee.

O God! Why in Thy name is
　Such allowed?
O God! Why always these
　Outside the crowd?

WHY DO I LOVE THIS COUNTRY

This is my country
And even though the soil of Georgia is dyed red,
And Florida's signs read "White only,"
They cannot keep from me the joy I feel
When peach trees bloom in early spring,
Or the warm delight which Florida's soft winds
bring.

And when I gaze over wide western plains
Lying at the foot of mountains
Like a mother's lap filled with her brood,
I can forget the ruthless men who bled
Upon these plains as the red men fled.

Or gazing from my window at the trees
With upstretched hands and faces to the sky,
I know again the self-same urge
Which makes men fight to live for their own country,
Or gives them unknown courage for their land to die.

So, when some man finds cause to ask:
"Why do you love this land?"
Quick to my lips the answer springs—
"Because I am a man!"

APRIL LONGING

This is too beautiful a day to walk alone,
To reach for you and fail to find you there;
To feel the April breeze caress my face,
And not to see that same wind brush your hair.

This is too beautiful a day to have to dream
Of how your face lights up, your soft eyes dance

At sight of crocus, marigolds, and roses,
Your sweet lips curved to kiss them with each glance.

It would be heavenly on such a day as this
To hear your laughter caught upon the breeze,
And follow with the wings of speed its curving course
Back to my heart, to bring its gift of ease.

Perhaps there is a reason for your absence,
Perhaps some purpose served when we're apart;
Perhaps. When Spring's bright flowers dress the land,
I only know I want you here against my heart.

Dolores Clinton

Dolores Clinton is 17 years old and a freshman in college.
She was feature editor of her high school paper. Both her
mother and father are teachers. This is her first published
poetry.

HERITAGE

Cotton swaying to and fro;
Backs, blistered and black, bent over.
Hands swiftly, noisily pulling at bolls.
Laughter and merriment drift from the porch
As a brother, under the skin,
Relaxes with cool juleps.

Anita Scott Coleman

Mrs. Coleman runs a children's boarding home in Los Angeles, Calif. She was born in Mexico and taught school for a while. Her poetry has appeared in the *Crisis, Opportunity, Negro Voices,* etc. She has been the recipient of several poetry awards.

AMERICA NEGRA

I am Indian;
I am grown old
Huddled beside sand dunes
Cradled in the lap of a plateau.
Cacti my shade,
Sky and land,
Land and sky,
The sky is clear as a mirror,
But the land is a painted desert;
Many the pictures I see there.
I am weary of seeing them. . . . . . .
Mirages of misery.

I am Irish and Scotch and Welsh,
Islands of rock,
Islands alone in the ocean,
Waves of the ocean bombarding;
Inflowing tides wash my shores,
Tides ebbing wash my shores clean,
Wash, wash mighty waters.
Is not England and France,
Germany and Spain,
Singapore and Shanghai in my veins?

Yes. . . . . .
I am Africa.
Africa stealing forth to meet
A lover in the everglades,
Chief Heartache,

Parleying with famine and sorrow
With never a war whoop.
Africa,
Singing the Irish caoine
Bewailing in accents of Scotland;
Mute are the harps;
Why are they voiceless?
Silent the bagpipes—
There was no victory.

I am Africa,
Africa the maiden;
My breasts are sweet apples;
My limbs are the flowering
Limbs of the fruit tree.
My body is fertile oasis
Alone in the barren desert,
Ever green in the sands of the desert.

In my veins the blood of all nations,
In my hands the jewels of all nations,
In my being the wisdoms and the passions of all
                              nations.
I am Africa
Rooted in America,
Africa the maiden,
Africa the conquered and the conqueror;
Beat, beat my heart
To the sound of the tom-toms;
Throb, throb my heart
To the roll of the drums.
Transplanted from Africa,
Nurtured in America,
Son of many races,
Fathered by many,
I am become
Man universal.

HANDS

Gnarled and knotty,
Iron-wrought hands,
Fashioned for the spade and plow,
Padded hard in calloused flesh
To rescind the spring of steel,
Hands . . . his, yours . . . mine,
Old black working-man's hands!
They wielded an ax felling trees
In new country,
They have tilled the soil of an alien land.
They have builded a house in an unfriendly habitat.
>Slender and lovely,
>Musical hands,
>Dusky in hue, fluttering over ivory keys
>Like a raven's wings;
>Do raven wings make music,
>Beating their way through inescapable air
>Mounting higher?

Hands, brown as snuff,
Wash-tub hands,
Curled like claws from clutching and squeezing
Heavy wet garments.
Water-soaked, sudsy, rheumy, old hands—
>Only when they are folded thus
>In the quiescent pose of death
>Are they stilled.

THE COLORIST

God is an Indian; He loves gay colors.
Red, yellow, orange are in the sky at sunset
And at the sunrise, too.
God is Irish. He loves green color best,
For all the trees and grasses in green garments
Ofttimes dress.

—50—

God is Saxon, stern and cold,
For snow is white and ice is cold,
The downy clouds are white, and a white moon peeks
When lovers pledge their troth.
Cotton is white, and snowy lambkin's fleece.
God is African. . . . . . .
For night is robed in black;
The twinkling stars are black men's eyes;
The black clouds tempests tell,
While little seeds of flowers birthed
Are tans and browns and black.

BLACK FACES

I love black faces:
   They are full of smouldering fire,
      And Negro eyes . . . white . . . with white desire,
      And Negro lips so soft and thick,
         Like rich velvet within fine jewelry cases.
I love black faces.

HUMILITY

They charge me with humility;
I who walk with a Humble One.
They taunt me, because to their eyes
I am poor;
I, who am daily fed!
They say:
I am lowly and poor and weak—
All of these things, they say,
Not knowing that my humility
Is the shadow cast,
The mighty shadow of a Humble One
In whose Hand my hand is clasped!

Jamye H. Coleman

Jamye Harris Coleman received her education at the Community School of Religion, Fisk University. She is the wife of a minister and mother of two children, one a Professor of English at Wilberforce University, the other a minister in Tennessee. She is the author of a book of poems, *Songs of My Soul;* a book of meditations, *Cries from the Cross,* and several plays.

IMPOSSIBILITY

The wit and laughter that stops
Thy tears
Cannot shatter the remorse
Of years.

No medical science can hold
The breath
When upon the patient is the hand
Of death.

Winds cannot change the course of
The sea,
And no one can fathom
Eternity.

THE SWING OF LIFE

Life is action,
Life is a song;
What is your theme
As you sing
To the throng?
How does it blend
As the path you trod;
Is it in tune
With the heart-beat of God?

—52—

William Cousins

A graduate of Yale University, Mr. Cousins taught Sociology for one year at Knoxville College. He is now studying for a Ph.D. in Sociology at the Yale Graduate School.

BLACK GAUNTLET

Yes, I dreamed once, as do all youth,
Of armour bright and stallion white
And odds o'ercome in valiant strife—
And so I sent my challenge out to Life
To find that he had challenged first—
And made me black.

ULTIMATUM

Mine is no plea for beggar's alms,
Nor mercy from my flailing fate.
I seek not wealth's deceptive charms,
Nor demagogue's imperiled estate.
I strive not even for your love;
I plead no longer—I demand
Your recognition—nothing more—
That black of skin, I am a man!

THE HOUSE OF TIME

I sit at the Desk of Death
In the Room of Now
In the House of Time.

The ever-slamming door to Then
Beats, beats against my tired brain—

The way it always has since
I first learned that Was was Was.
My soul peers through the window
At Eternity, and strains—impatient—
In the narrow confines of my body.

But I must wait my turn
At the Desk of Death
In the Room of Now
In the House of Time.

Frank Marshall Davis

Frank Marshall Davis is Executive Editor of the Associated
Negro Press, and Editor of the Chicago *Star;* former Rosenwald Fellow in poetry; author of *Black Man's Verse, I Am
the American Negro,* and a new volume of verse, *47th Street,*
now in the hands of the publisher. He has contributed poetry
and prose to periodicals and anthologies too numerous to
enumerate. Several of his pieces appeared in *Negro Voices.*

PEACE IS A FRAGILE CUP

I sing for the silent slain
Speak for the dogtagged dead
Soldiers shorn of expendable lives
Civilians cold among shattered stones
I am their voice shouting for a living peace.

We have come a long way, historians say
Cave to skyscrapper, oxcart to plane
But what does it profit a man
Penicillin-saved from pneumonia yesterday
Only to die today by an atom bomb?

Pithecanthropus erectus to homo mechanicus
Runs the saga of science
Maker of stone tools to smasher of atoms

(Flint-tipped arrows to block busters)
Master of mass production
(Recall Nazi gas chambers at Lublin)
Enslaver of the sky
(Lunch in London, afternoon flights over Belgrade)
Who kicked civilization into the street
Changing her
To a quarter prostitute?

The silent slain speak a common tongue
The dogtagged dead hymn a similar song
This man's peace is signed with a wooden cross
One war ends each time a soldier dies
Fighting there has always been
The lonesome warrior fighting the lonely fight
The centipede army smashing the multi-armed foe
Blood and brains spattered on impersonal soil
The hounds of hate baying and biting
Thermopylae, Gettysburg, Bataan
Repeating
Like a continuous performance
At the cinema citadels—

Because this ever was
Must it always be?

You have to hand it to the experts
They've got it all figured out
Safe in their Home Offices
It costs exactly this much to kill a man
To equip an army such a size
Means so many billion dollars in contracts
And the profits are good—
No fighting for markets
No high-powered advertising campaign—
Deliver and get paid.
(Buddy, how much folding stuff
Have you left from your war plant job?
Soldier, which was closer:

The long green or the green earth?)
And after it's all over
Look at the pile you've made!
And you're left with a bigger factory
To make more, sell more.
Move in where the armies fought yesterday
And clean up—
They've got it all figured out—
If they forget Hiroshima. . .

I say
We have not been left among the living
To become a new generation of dying
They who survived at Stalingrad
Do not covet the breath
Of the untouched millions in Chicago.

Peace was a fragile set of chinaware
But in this day of the atom bomb
Only one thin cup remains.
Take it then
From the careless fists
Of the money drunk.
Place it in the reaching hands,
The safe-wishing anxious hands,
Of the little people
So that they may set it
Gently
Behind glass doors in the cupboard
And point proudly to visitors
On an endless chain of calm tomorrows
Saying,
"Look, there it is.
It's been in the family
For years!"

MISS SAMANTHA WILSON

In her sixtieth year
Miss Samantha Wilson,
Recluse and religious,
Suddenly as a dictator making new laws,
Turned from the wilted loneliness
Of her dejected brown cottage,
Companionship of two pious cats,
Mothership of a mannerly brood of potted plants,
And moved among the ailing townspeople
Hovering all night
Beside the beds of the deathly sick
Like an aged angel,
Bathing souls with purple prayers,
Refusing to leave before life left,
And the town that had known her
Only as a name and a gray-haired virgin
Now praised her unselfishness,
Shared its most fragile secrets
And erected its new hospital in her honor.

But it was not for these things
That Samantha Wilson labored.

Knowing death eyed her closely,
Dreading eternity friendless,
She was arranging for companions
Among the fatally sick she'd tended
To be watchfully waiting
In that misty place
Beyond the grave.

H. Binga Dismond

Dr. H. Binga Dismond, a native of Richmond, Va., is Director of the Department of Physical Therapy at the Harlem Hospital in New York, doing original work in the field. During his college years he was a celebrated track star, setting several records in the field. He is a Chevalier of the National Order of Honor and Merit of Haiti, having been cited by President Stenio Vincent for his work following the Dominican massacre of 1937.

REVOLT IN THE SOUTH

I shall knock at your kitchen window no more;
I shall walk right up to your very front door;
And no matter what your greeting be,
I shall not "Mister" you unless you "Mister" me.

TO THE MEN OF THE SOVIET ARMY

Mother, what's a Red?
A Red, my son, is one
Who died that you might live—
When Aryan hordes and Fascist lords
Denied that God had right to give
Liberty to you and me.

THE DOMINICAINE

It was on that night down by the bay
On the road that leads to Bizoton,
The palms were waving to the sea
And lights in the town had just come on.
Up in the sombre Haitian Hills

The drums had started up again—
And you would have done just what I did
Had you seen the Dominicaine.

I sipped my rum and *café noir*
And, hopeful, watched her dark brown eyes.
She smiled at me from where she sat;
I had been right in my surmise.
And then we danced a slow *meringue;*
The drums kept up their dull refrain—
And you would have done just what I did
Had you kissed the Dominicaine.

I've traveled far through the Caribe—
From Ponce down to Curacao.
But memories of that Haitian night
Still dog my steps wherever I go.
Her burning kisses seared my lips;
Those drums could drive a man insane—
But you would have done just what I did
Had you loved the Dominicaine.

Elroy Douglas

Elroy Douglas served in both World War I and II. He studied
at Tuskegee Institute Auto Mechanics School, and has been
writing poetry for over twenty years. He lives in Brooklyn,
New York.

THIS DAY

This day is mine. I greet the dawn
And pledge a willing hand
To do my best unto the end
To help my fellow man.

The service I propose to give
May seem so very small,

But someone weak and sore oppressed
Needs rescue from a fall.

Tomorrow's sun is never sure . . .
I know not when nor how.
There is no cause to wait or choose;
The time to help is now.

This day is mine. And when the dawn
Has changed to setting sun,
My aim will be achieved because
This day was well begun.

Ylessa Dubonee

Ylessa Duboneé is a resident of California. During the war
she worked in various USO centers throughout the country.
She has traveled extensively in Canada and Mexico, and is
now studying radio writing.

DEPARTURE

This mirror that reflects me, cool, serene,
Knows nothing of the turmoil in my mind;
It does not show that I recall the scene
Of your departure. It reflects how kind
The years have been to me to leave no trace
Of what has been my life. No indication
Of nights of longing lies upon my face;
No sign is there of your love's revelation.
Yet in my mind I hear impassioned words,
Yield to your arms, and feel your burning kiss;
Still I hear singing of a thousand birds
And know the sweet oblivion of bliss.

Each moment in my heart these memories burn . .
Each memory is a prayer for your return.

NOCTURNE

Last night I went out into the moonlight,
Into the soft, silvery moonlight.
The magic orb was casting
    Streamers of soft translucent silver
    Among the silhouetted trees . . .
The brilliant stars enhanced my loneliness—
Then suddenly I wished that I might be
    Close, close, in your arms . . .
My mind's mouth savoured your hot, dewy kisses,
And the body of my thoughts felt
    Your caressing hands . . .

For a moment only I stood in loneliness
    Too intense for me to bear.
Then I reentered my room and beckoned you
    Into my waking dreams . . .

James A. Emanuel

James A. Emanuel was confidential secretary to Brig. General
Benjamin O. Davis for two years, until his entrance into the
Army. He served overseas in the Philippines and Netherlands
East Indies, and was discharged in July, 1946. He is at pres-
ent a sophomore at Howard University in Washington, D. C.

DEFEAT

I loathe defeat, whose keen-edged plow
Furrows deep my heart, where springs the weed
So quickly grown to monstrous height—
Abhorréd plant of an odious seed.

Its poignant barb pursues me far,
Like Io driven by the fly,
And shame-embodied fetters reach
From every part of earth and sky.

No man could make of me the slave
Defeat commands with shadowed glance;
No chance combine of passions' end
Could anguish in like circumstance.

But perhaps this grim chastiser
Serves me in his truceless might,
Exciting my imprisoned self
To break its bonds and seek the light.

John W. Fentress

John Wesley Fentress is a graduate of Tuskegee Institute
where he was class poet. He taught at A. & M. College in
Alabama, at the Topeka (Kans.) Educational Institute, and
in a boarding school for Indians and Negroes in Oklahoma.
He has worked as reporter on the Montgomery (Ala.)
Tribune, the Associated Negro Press, and the Pittsburgh
Courier. At present he conducts his own commercial art
studio in Norfolk, Va., and is working on a collection of his
verse.

BOOKER T. WASHINGTON

He taught his race to labor and to wait
As Moses taught while leading Israel's host;
They heard, and gently spread from coast to coast
That idea whereon hangs this nation's fate—
Happy must be that people and that state
Whose lofty privilege it is to boast
Kinship with one whose lifework meant the most
To prove that only those who serve are great.
The system which he shaped is world-approved,
Although this granite rock his body hides.
Here on these green hills fair and far removed,
The beauty of his spirit still abides.
The onl spirit that can make men free—
Spirit of faith and love—that's Booker T.

ABRAHAM LINCOLN

You came upon us in our darkest hour,
As we were kneeling, praying, half in doubt;
It seemed that even God had left us out
Beyond the reaches of His saving power.
Then strangely down from heaven like a shower
Your great love fell, and put our foes to rout.
Up from the nation's lips there rose a shout
Of praise that lingers to this very hour!

To conquer, you were not too proud to stoop—
If stooping might a drifting nation save.
The heavy burden made your shoulders droop;
You died to free the master and the slave.

You came upon us in our darkest hour;
Death left you standing like a rugged tower.

Catherine L. Finley

An elementary school teacher in Birmingham, Alabama, Mrs.
Finley began writing poetry in high school, and says that her
greatest inspiration came "when I was asked by one of my
high school teachers to recite a poem by a famous poet. Un-
able to recall one at the moment, I recited one of my own,
naming William Cullen Bryant as the poet. She accepted it.
To this day I don't know if the poem was that good or the
teacher that stupid."

ICICLES ON TREES

The moon saw
Blowing wind
Breathe cold upon their dripping boughs,
Chilling their nude limbs
In the midst of silent sighs.

PERCEPTION

I like the way you look at things—
A wintered oak or budding rose.
Never just a rugged oak with mossy beard,
But Time's infinite arm grown strong;
Not just a bud unfolding in the sun,
Ah, but the smiling face of God you see.
I like the way you look at things,
Yes, even at me.

Francis M. Foster

Ist Lt. Francis Merrill Foster is a dentist now serving in the
U. S. Army. His poetry has appeared in the Pittsburgh
Courier, People's Voice and other papers. His last letter was
from Guam.

HUNGER

Just for a moment of your love I crave,
This weakened starveling yearning for a taste
Of gentle moments one night you gave . . .
. . . . the particles of Life never to waste.
Pass down the portion to the famished slave
And pray he does not choke in eager haste.

A LOVER'S LAMENT

I never dreamed that we would drift apart
And now I dare to think my fate unreal.
You left a dagger tearing at my heart;
I hunger for the touch of lips that heal.

L. Zack Gilbert

L. Zack Gilbert worked during World War II in one of the Chicago war plants. His home is in Cairo, Illinois, and he is now working on a volume of poetry.

LONG, BLACK LINE

There's a long, black line
A-waiting for freedom;
Long, black line's a-waiting.
There's a long, black line
Striving for freedom;
Striving and fighting
For freedom.

No more crossing the river of Jordan;
No more crossing into camp ground;
No more giving their all for heaven;
No more waiting till the trumpet sounds.

They gonna give their all, their all for freedom
For that's their glory chair.
So come on down, sweet Jesus, come along—
Gonna make their heaven here.

We are a long, black line
A-waiting for freedom;
Long, black line's a-waiting.
We are a long, black line
Striving for freedom;
Striving and fighting
For freedom.

We gonna give the all, the all for freedom,
For that's our glory chair.
So come on down, sweet Jesus, come along—
Gonna make our heaven here.

We are a long, black line
Striving for freedom,
Striving and fighting
For an equal share.

Lenora Gillison

This is the first published work of Mrs. Gillison. She is a
mother and housewife living in Richmond, Virginia.

SUPREMACY

Pain—
Sharp, gnawing, comes
Like a storm-fed mountain flood,
And goes suddenly
Like a flash across the blue.
Slumber—
A blanket of forgetfulness
Covers her, blotting out the pain,
Until the budding life sheltered within
Stretches forth again to grasp
Eagerly, yet hesitantly,
At fulfilment.
Pain—
More pain, sharper, swifter.
The Valley of the Shadow looms ahead.
The Reaper beckons.
She gives no sign that she has seen.
Bravely she labors to keep
That which he would take,
Bearing the pain that promises life,
Defying Death.
Pain—
Final, unrelenting pain.
Triumphantly she leaves the Vale
Crowned with Motherhood!

Ruby Berkley Goodwin

Ruby Berkley Goodwin, writer, lecturer and teacher, is a former Hollywood correspondent and private secretary to Hattie McDaniel, the actress. The author of three published books, *Twelve Negro Spirituals* (in collaboration with William Grant Still), *From My Kitchen Window*, a volume of verse; and *A Gold Star Mother Speaks*, a narrative poem, she has completed work on a fictionized biography, *It's Fun to Be Black*.

IF THIS BE GOOD-BYE

If this be good-bye,
Let it be said softly and sweetly,
As though it were the parting of a few hours.
There should be no tears that tighten the throat;
No look of anguish in tired eyes.

If this be good-bye,
Let it be said gaily and bravely,
As though tomorrow held no dark room
Of terrifying loneliness. There will be
Other nights for crying and pillows for tears
But they come after parting,
Not with it, my love.

NEW YEAR'S PRAYER

Help me to make my heart a citadel,
High on a sunlit hill where love and faith hold sway;
Help me to guard the drawbridge to my heart,
And when dark clouds of hate or greed or malice
                              come my way,
To close the passage quickly,
Leaving myself untouched by poisoned breath.

Help me to know that men in every land
Love sunlight more than darkness,
Love music more than wailing shrieks of bombs,
Love handclasps more than piercing thrust of steel;
And though prudence decrees dark streets, dark
                              homes,
Dark cities in our land—
Let there be no blackout of love in my own heart,
For any of Thy children, God, I pray.

GUILTY

*(A Negro soldier was killed by a bus driver in a
southern state because he did not know the jim crow
section of the car)*

I did not know my place—
That is the crime for which I died.
I did not know where to sit,
Or how to bow low,
Or when to say "Yes, sir." to Mr. George.

I grew up with stardust in my eyes,
Stardust gathered from a million
Hopes and dreams of great men
Who died to make this a strong free nation.

True, all was not stardust.
I remembered Jamestown, Virginia,
And Harper's Ferry.
But a war was fought to end the shame
Of human slavery, or so I was told
By my teachers in New York.

I became a man and I heard
Of the Four Freedoms,
How good they sounded to me:
Freedom from want,

No more breadlines,
No more Salvation Army clothes,
No more relief doles,
No more hard-boiled case workers.

Freedom to worship,
I could sing "Steal Away" and "Ave Maria"
On Beale Street or in Carnegie Hall.
I could serve an invisible God
Or worship an image of gold or brass.

Freedom of speech,
I could laugh with Rochester on the radio,
Disagree with the Dies committee,
Yell for the Brooklyn Dodgers,
Or criticize the President.

And freedom from fear.
That was the greatest freedom
Of them all;
For the man who has no fear
Is the only free man in the world.

I wrapped the Four Freedoms around me
When I put on my uniform
And started south to become a soldier
To save the world from tyranny.

But I did not know my place—
That is the crime for which I died.
I did not know where to sit,
Or how to bow low,
Or when to say "Yes, sir." to Mr. George.

WE LAUNCHED A SHIP

On one never-to-be-forgotten day, we launched a ship.
The full-throated voice of Marian Anderson

proclaimed,
"I christen thee Booker T. Washington."
A bottle broke and champagne sprayed the prow
Of the giant liberty ship as she slid proudly down the
ways
And sat serenely on the broad face of the ocean.

We launched a ship and the proud workers
Both black and white stood together and cheered.
They cheered with throats suddenly gone tight
And smiled at each other with eyes blurred
By the happy tears that trembled on lashes,
Or were brushed quickly aside by a calloused hand.

We launched a ship and the captain stood proudly on
its deck.
He was a Negro, fearless and soft-spoken,
He breathed deeply and said to his crew,
"This ship—our ship—is more than a ship.
It is a symbol—a symbol of the dream that is
America.
We must never let that dream die.

We launched a ship and the crew looked at their
captain.
Some have called it a strange crew,
For the men were from many countries,
But all were bound by the love of freedom
And a fervent belief in the equality of man;
So the crew looked at their captain,
Black, brown, yellow, and white faces
Looked at the captain.
They answered not in words but each heart said,
"We know—we know—that's why we are here!"

The Captain's voice was silent but his heart asked
back,
"And why are you here?"
Their hearts responded,

"Because all men are brothers,
Because black and white workers will
Work together in harmony,
Because there is a place in the world
For black leadership."

The shouting of the crowd on shore
Beat against the hull of the ship.
The black and white workers on the pier said proudly,
"We worked together to build her."
The black and white crew aboard resolved,
"We'll work together and sail her."

We launched a ship—
A ship with a glorious mission,
And it became the symbol of a
Dawning brotherhood throughout the world.

Myrtle Campbell Gorham

Myrtle Campbell Gorham was born in Boston and worked
as stenographer in the department of Public Welfare there.
She lived in New York for three years, during which time
she was a member of the James Weldon Johnson Literary
Guild. She is married and lives in Washington, D. C. Her
poetry has appeared in *The Crisis*, Boston *Chronicle* and
Associated Negro Press.

SERVICE, PLEASE

Dear God, when you send your angels out to do their
                              chores tonight,
Bid one of them dust well my star of hope.
For many anxious nights in vain I've peered,
Only to see a cloud where once it shone so bright.

My wagon waits below,
Filled to the brim with things of which I may well be
                              proud,
But please, dear God, I need the power of my star
To draw the heavy load.

William Thompson Goss

William Thompson Goss served for two years in the U. S.
Navy during World War I and afterwards studied art in
Paris. Upon his return to America he worked as commercial
artist for the Chevrolet Motor Company. He is now devoting
all of his time to writing.

MAN TO MAN

Oh, come my brother of the fairer skin
And lean on me. Why must you shy away
At my approach? Come, let me take your hand.
The weight of wealth and power have stymied your
Approach to peace; your charted course has been
Deflected by sadistic bigotry.
Do lean on me; my strength has not been spent
In toilsome preachments that my lineage is
Superior. In time you too shall come
To recognize the utter fallacy
Of "super race" and "white supremacy."
The worst of our complexes shall dissolve
When we behold each other in the light,
And find that both can be acceptable.

VARIETY

The dormant mind's essential stimulus
Is but the essence of variety
Which holds an oft distorted truth for us:

That beauty does not of necessity
Conform to one specific shape, or size,
Or one specific color of a thing.
Beyond the purple mist the mountains rise
To beauty which compels the heart to sing
A roundelay which might as well etxol
The simple beauty of a vine-clad knoll.

Unfurling petals struggling to be
A rose are no less beautiful to see.

And "I am black but comely," even so
Sang Solomon a long, long time ago.

Emily Jane Greene

Emily Jane Greene lives in Los Angeles, and is employed by
the State of California in the Division of Apprenticeship
Standards. She was graduated from the Los Angeles City
College and for a time was playground director for the Los
Angeles Board of Education. She has worked as columnist
for the California *Eagle* and reporter on the Eagle's Radio
newscast, and is the author of several religious plays presented
in Los Angeles.

HE'S COMING HOME AT LAST

There were hours and many of valor,
And many were those of suspense,
There were hours and many of terror,
While he fought for the Nation's defense.

There were hours and many of courage
While seeking a hidden mine,
And many hours of tension,
Were spent on the banks of the Rhine.

There were hours and many of bloodshed,
The loss of many and many a man,
There were hours and many of heartaches,
Before the fall of Japan.

There were hours and many, blood curdling,
Beneath a smoky and fiery sky,
And hours of fear and bewilderment
While he waited, expecting to die.

There were hours and many of exhaustion,
Exposure, and also despair,
With no time for relaxation,
There was not a moment to spare.

There were hours and many in battle,
When a buddy would stumble and fall,
When mechanically he did his job,
Though his heart wasn't in it at all.

The hours and many of struggle
Are now echoes that speak of the past,
For the fog of the tumult has lifted,
And he's coming home at last.

Amos J. Griffin

Corporal Amos J. Griffin is a skilled Surgical Technician in
the Army Air Forces stationed at Keesler Field, Miss. His
last year at Leland College in Baton Rouge, La., was inter-
rupted by his entrance into the Army. This is his first published poetry.

SALUTE TO THE TAN YANKS

From the shores of the Atlantic
To the wide Pacific's blue,
We have done our share of fighting;

We have shed our life's blood, too.
Can you show me just one campaign
That a Tan Yank did not see,
Putting in his bid for freedom,
Dying to set men free?
No you can't! We fought and sweated
Till the whole days' work was done;
And we helped to bear the burden
Till the holocaust was won.
Italy, France, and then the Rhineland,
We fought there side by side,
And Death played his hand indifferent:
Both the White and Tan Yanks died.
We marched through the South Sea Islands
Till our weary feet were sore;
You were there; you saw us take it;
Heard us make those big guns roar.
Suddenly . . . the guns were silent . . .
Shouts of triumph filled the air.
"War is over! War is over!"
Answer to the mothers' prayer.
It was on the homebound "V-ships"
That you drew the color line;
"Black men separate from White men,
Every color to its kind!"
Can't you hear those brave men clamor?
Can't you hear our heroes call?
"We died for the cause of freedom,
Liberty and life for all."
Would you do us the injustice . . .
Falling in the same old track,
Limit us our rightful freedom
Just because our skin is Black?
Rise up Men! Declare with fervor that:
"All prejudice must cease!
We fought hard for *other's* freedom.
Now we'll fight to make *our* peace."

Carlyle B. Hall

Born and educated in Washington, D. C., Mr. Hall began
writing poetry while serving in the Army in World War II.
He resides in New York City with his wife and two children.

I WAKE UP SCREAMING

I see the blinding flash once more
And hear again the hellish roar
And see the twisted bodies strewed
All over hell's half-acres.
Men from every walk of life,
Doctors, lawyers, bakers,
Each one doomed in the maddening plight
To give their lives, not willingly,
To satisfy Mars' appetite:
Blood and guts all strewed about
As though it were some human dump.
Then my flesh grows creepy cold
And my throat acquires a lump,
And before I realize I'm dreaming,
Once again I wake up screaming.

MALEVOLENCE

The body on the magnolia tree swung slowly in a
                    measured tread
And crazy rhythmic motions made;
A human body, black and dead.
Above the sweet and sickening smell of the magnolia
                    and the rosebud,
There wafts upon the scented air the sweet and
                    sickening smell of blood;
"Southern honor" has been avenged by deed both
                    "brave" and "bold."
The proof: that hanging body there
Broken, cut, and cold.

The murdering horde had gone its way, proud of a
    "Southern deed."
The broken body sobs, "Some day . . ."
And an answering voice says, "Yes, my son.
For this one thing fate has decreed:
Whatever you do, wherever you go,
Somewhere on life's highway the piper must be paid.
For as you have reaped—so shall you sow."

SOLITUDE

I sit here by the fire and watch the dying embers
And think of all the time gone by—
Junes, Julys, Novembers:
Lonely days without you; the nights so long and cold.
Then the whistling wind breathes your name
And tears my very soul.
The final embers glow anew to try and put the dark
    to rout
And glitter like a diamond till a teardrop puts them
    out.
Then the darkness seems to rush me, and it wrecks
    my very mind—
And I cry just as a woman would, for the love I
    left behind.

Helen C. Harris

Helen C. Harris, a graduate of St. Augustine's College and Boston University, is co-author of *Triad,* a book of verse. During the war she was employed as Engineer's Assistant in the Signal Corps Development Laboratory; she has returned to teaching and writing.

I HEARD YOUR HEART'S SOFT TEARS

In the lightness of the breeze
I heard your heart's soft tears
Drop—one by one—upon a rim.
They balanced there, then fell
Into the pool of life
And welded there
A part of something called tomorrow's dream.

There are so many tears that you have wept
In laughter, awe, in trepidation.
Never, some say, have you learned to cry—
Your wings forever upward fly,
Strong, whipping against wind and time.
How would others know of anguish in your heart?
Inside the pulse of night,
Outside the door of yesterday,
I heard a sigh—and ran to let you in,
Only to find the silent one who stood outside
Was I.

SPIN ME A DREAM

Spin me a dream, weaver of my soul,
And let me wear it for just a day.
Let me parade with uplifted head
Before the throng so free, so gay.

Spin me a dream from finest stuff
And fashion it exquisitely bold.
For the rags I wear are colorless, torn,
And my heart is naked and cold.

TO THE SINGER

Sing the song the winter's way—
The tune is quick and white;
The stars are cold,
The trees are strong and bare.

Sing the song the winter's way
Sharpened hard and clear;
The theme is crisp,
The melody empty air.

Sing the song the winter's way,
But be remembering
The words are hidden deep—so deep
Within the heart of spring.

Edna L. Harrison

Edna L. Harrison, a native of Boston, Mass., is of British West Indian parentage. She has been teacher, factory worker, settlement house worker, office worker, handicraft worker and newspaper reporter. At present she is specializing in handicraft, making costume jewelry and lapel yarn dolls. She also writes interviews for the Boston *Chronicle*. Her poetry has appeared in numerous periodicals.

FIRST LADY
(*To Mrs. Eleanor Roosevelt*)

The real warmth is in her smile,
And the way she shakes your hand,

With a firm and friendly grasp,
As though she can understand
The things men live and die for
To make a better life
That's free from hate and torture,
Race prejudice and strife.

She is the world's "First Lady,"
Who lifts her voice again
For peace on earth, good will and
Real freedom for *all* men.

Samuel A. Haynes

A native of Belize, British Honduras, Mr. Haynes is a journalist, writer and interracial worker. He is copy editor of the Afro-American Newspapers, Inc., in Baltimore. Veteran of World War I, he has travelled extensively in Europe, Asia, the West Indies, Central America, Canada and tne United States, and was former confidential secretary and personal representative of the late Marcus Garvey. He has contributed to *Opportunity,* the *African,* etc., and was former Associate Editor of the *Negro World,* Virginia Peninsula Editor-Manager of the Norfolk (Va.) *Journal and Guide,* and editorial staff-member of the Philadelphia *Tribune.*

WARNING

Listen, white man,
Listen well:

We who are black and courageous
No longer cry, nor cringe,
Nor run to rocks to hide our faces
When justice is betrayed,
Democracy crucified;
For this know—
There's no hiding place
From prejudice and hate.

No longer are we prone to hide
When Klansmen burn a cross
Or retreat ignominiously
From racial bigots who,
Fearing truth, rule by force
And intimidation,
And substitute moral law
For the law of the jungle.

This we also know—
That freedom is not won
By running from but by facing up
To the bigots who would make freedom
A gift none other must receive
But you who are white.
This we are resolved to do
Today, henceforth.

So, whitewash, exonerate your lynchers,
Turn loose your Klan and Columbians
Upon us who are black;
Unleash your Fascist terrors;
Do the worst of which you are capable
In your mad determination
To "keep us in our places"
And make white supremacy work.

But when you are through
With this mockery of freedom,
This blasphemy against God,
Truth and human decency,
When you shall have spent
Your revelry in the muck and slime
Of mob rule and intolerance,
You will be spent and beaten because:

We who are black and courageous
Will still be here, will survive,
Just as our sires survived slavery.

Your sadistic impulses,
Your barbaric practices,
The bullets and blackjacks of your policemen
Will never crush our will to be free
And equal with all Americans, all men.

Listen, white man,
Listen well:

We who are black and courageous
Will not retreat one inch
In the uncompromising struggle
For unqualified citizenship
And the protection of our life and property.
We shall stand where we are—
Stand, and fight, and die
Until we are free Americans, equal with all men.

THE CHALLENGE

Climb high, black boy,
Climb high;
The world owes you no more
Than what you wrest from it.

Dream on, black boy,
Dream on;
Everything around you
Was born of dreams.

Think straight, black boy,
Think straight;
The difference between masters and slaves
Is a difference of mind.

Work hard, black boy,
Work hard;

The honest toiler
Is a prince in his own right.

Have faith, black boy,
Have faith;
You and God can win
Against the odds.

Be brave, black boy,
Be brave;
If you win or lose,
Do so valiantly.

You can lead a nation,
Black boy,
Or remain a slave—
Yours the will, the deed.

Gene Holmes

Gene Holmes was born in Liberia, West Africa, of missionary
parents. She came to the United States five years ago to study
at Hampton Institute and New York University, an M.D.
being her objective. Her poetry has been published in Liberia,
and translated in Sweden. She has a novel ready for publication on life in Liberia, and is now at work on another.

THE GOLDEN STOOL

O Sky God,
Ruler of sky and land,
Send us in our distress
An Ark of Covenant.

We, thy people of Ashanti,
Have suffered long at the
Hands of tyranny and barbarism

From conquerors of strange hues.
They come in great ships
Manned by powerful guns,
Lured by our gold
And envious of our solidarity,
Our well organized trade
And the intelligence of our Seers.
They come to take captive our women.
They steal upon us at night
When we are at rest,
When new children are being created
And our sons and daughters are making
Merry in the moonlight, and love is eager.
They come in the name of
One Great White Queen
Who wishes to rule us, and to reduce
The ancient dynasty of our kings,
Our heritage, and our lores,
To filth.

O Sky God,
We, thy people of Ashanti,
Are weak and weary of strife.
Five times have we fought
These barbarians across the sea.
Our land and cities have been turned
Into a cesspool of corruption:
Where brother eats brother,
While sister looks on, too moved to weep.
Our sons and daughters
Who once took pride in the
Soil of their fathers
Now sell themselves in the streets of Kumasi
For a bowl of rice.
Our fields that once waved with yellow harvest
Are now black-charred earth.
Our great art and civilization
Has been stolen and destroyed.
Now we must pay huge indemnities

To men whom we owe nothing
Save the ruin of our hearths;
We must borrow back from them
Of our own wealth
So that we may crown our king
Who was ruling us in wisdom and peace
When these barbarians were still in caves.
Our royal family is threatened
With banishment to an unknown land,
While we, their children, are left
In the hands of an unkind people.
Help us, O Sky God!

Two thousand years ago
Our fathers were assembled before the sacred rock
With sacrifices, beseeching help from the gods
When lo, the skies became dark
And the great hills shook with fear,
And the small hills trembled with uncertainty.
The streams grew silent;
The birds flapped their wings
Aimlessly in the thick darkness;
And out of the blackness a rumbling was heard,
And still another, and yet a louder rumbling
Ten times as powerful as the British guns.
And out of the rumbling, which clogged our ears,
Our hearts heard the Voice of Thee,
Great Sky God, declaring us Thy people.

Now, now the skies over Ashanti are dark again,
Dark with the hovering of the oppressors, yes,
But darker yet with the omen of approaching help.
Our Sand Cutters and Seers prophesied
That when this omen returned,
With it would come one Anotchi,
A bearer of good tidings.
Bring out the loud drums;
Bring out the gourds and small wailing drums
From their hiding places;

Come, all ye children of Ashanti;
Come out of the ruins of Kumasi;
Come from your hiding places
In the mountains and caves;
Come from the thick forest and beside cool streams.
Wash and oil your bodies with palm oil and cinnamon.
Come clad in garments of yellow and white and gold.
Bring your wives and sons and daughters;
Bring the crippled and blind and lame.
Your salvation is here:

Out of the rumbling which clogged their ears,
Out of the lightning which blinded their eyes;
Their hearts heard once more
The soothing voice of the Sky God,
Delivering to his people his Covenant.
When the mist was rolled away,
Their eyes beheld a sacred golden stool
Ten times brighter than the noon-day sun.

Out of the distance came the voice of Anotchi
As he ascended into the ancient hills:
"From this time forward, O men of Ashanti,
The Golden Stool shall be your most sacred
                                possession.
It shall make thee a great and powerful people;
Even the king shall be second to it.
Guard it with your sacred fires.
And peace be with thee!"

Langston Hughes

Langston Hughes has been publishing poetry since 1921. His first book, *The Weary Blues,* was issued in 1926. Since that time he has devoted himself to writing and lecturing. He was awarded a Guggenheim Fellowship in 1935 and a Rosenwald Fellowship in 1940. His play, "Mulatto," was produced on Broadway, and his lyrics for the musical version of Elmer Rice's "Street Scene" have been acclaimed. He has also written a novel, a collection of short stories, articles, part of an autobiography and several other plays. His fifth book of poems, *Fields of Wonder,* was published in early 1947.

FOR BILLIE HOLIDAY

What can purge my heart
  Of the song
  And the sadness?
What can purge my heart
  But the song
  Of the sadness?
What can purge my heart
  Of the sadness
  Of the song?

Do not speak of sorrow
With dust in her hair,
Or bits of dust in eyes
A chance wind blows there.
The sorrow that I speak of
Is dusted with despair.

Voice of muted trumpet.
Cold brass in warm air.
Bitter television blurred
By sound that shimmers—
  Where?

WISDOM AND WAR

We do not care—
That much is clear.
Not enough
Of us care
Anywhere.

We are not wise—
For that reason,
Mankind dies.

To think
Is much against
The will.

Better—
And easier—
To kill.

FROM SELMA

In places like
Selma, Alabama,
Kids say,
 In places like
 Chicago and New York . . . . .
In places like
Chicago and New York
Kids say,
 In places like
 London and Paris . . . . .
In places like
London and Paris
Kids say,
 In places like
 Chicago and New York . . . . .

Lois Royal Hughes

Lois Royal Hughes, daughter of a Methodist minister, made her formal bow in book form in *Negro Voices*. Married and living in Cape May, N. J., she is completing a book of poetry.

RENDEZVOUS

I had a rendezvous with love
Along the primrose way.
Love seemed to me so very sweet
I gave my heart away.
I planned another rendezvous
When love and I could meet;
Love came and went, but left my heart
In ashes at my feet.

LIKE UNTO A ROSE

I tried to pattern all my life
Like the petals of a rose,
With fragrance delicately pure
Where dust found no repose.
And though the raindrops often fall
Or harsh breezes blow,
Not rain nor wind destroyed the bud
Because you willed it so.

But I forgot when roses bloom,
Their petals fade and die,
So often leaving only thorns
To prick some passer-by.
So if the bloom you loved is dead
And thorns are all you see,
Perhaps the fragrance will remain,
Reminding you of me.

I COULD NOT KNOW

I thought that missing you would fall
At close of every day
As shadows fall across the sun
To chase the light away.
I thought that missing you might flood
The hours that I should sleep
As ocean waves rise over the sand
Or beat against the deep.
I thought that missing you would grow
Against the darkened sky
As friendly trees grow ghostly weird
And breezes seem to sigh.

I could not know that missing you,
Like thunderstorms in May,
Could cut across the noontime task
In such a frightening way.
I could not know that missing you
When someone else is near,
Could still a voice, leaving me deaf
To voices loud and clear.
I could not know that missing you,
I'd hear you call my name
In crowded rooms or empty halls
And answer you the same.

Dorothy Vena Johnson

Dorothy Vena Johnson teaches Creative English in the Los Angeles High Schools. She is founder-president of the Allied Arts League, and Treasurer of the Los Angeles Creative Writing Teachers Association. Her poetry has been published in numerous anthologies, including *Negro Voices,* and magazines.

EPITAPH FOR A BIGOT

Life to the bigot is a whip
That lashes creed and laity;
Here lies the one who lost his grip
And cringed to Death—a refugee.

POST WAR BALLAD

If Crispus Attuck's statue
    Took life to walk,
He would wink his owl-eyes,
    Part lips and talk.
"What of the country for which
    I shed first blood?
Did freedom blossom
    From our small bud?"

He would journey down
    To Washington
To trace the democracy
    The war had begun.
"How wide was the pathway?
    What of my race?
Do they freedom
    Fully embrace?"

"Have there been other wars
  Since when I fell?
Are there any memorials
  For blacks who excel?"
He would proudly look
  For murals on the wall
Telling the story
  All in all.

Shaking his weary head
  With a slight frown,
He would trek on back
  To Boston-town.
There, hearing how Nazis
  Brewed some evil deeds,
And how his loyal race
  Was disdained like weeds,

He would sadly bow his head,
  Feeling sad and alone,
And quietly say, "I guess
  I would better stay a stone."

ROAD TO ANYWHERE

Defeat is not to lose,
  Nor to despair;
Defeat may be a road
  To anywhere.

SUCCESS

Success is like a blazing flame
  Of meteoric light;
The sparks may glow eternally
  Or vanish over-night.

Georgia Douglas Johnson

Georgia Douglas Johnson is the author of three books of verse, several plays and songs, a novel and a biography. A new book of verse is being published in England.

I'VE LEARNED TO SING

I'v learned to sing a song of hope;
I've said good-bye to despair;
I caught the note in a thrush's throat;
I sang, and the world was fair.

I've learned to sing a song of joy—
It bends the skies to me;
The song of joy is the song of hope
Grown to maturity.

I've learned to laugh away my tears
As through the dark I go,
That love and laughter conquer fears
My heart has come to know.

I've learned a song of happiness—
It is the song of love,
For love alone is happiness
And happiness is love!

INTERRACIAL

Let's build bridges here and there
Or, sometimes, just a spiral stair
That we may come somewhat abreast
And sense what cannot be expressed,
And by these measures can be found
A meeting place—a common ground
Nearer the reaches of the heart

Where truth revealed, stands clear, apart;
With understanding come to know
What laughing lips will never show:
How tears and torturing distress
May masquerade as happiness;
Then you will know when my heart's aching
And I when yours is slowly breaking;

Commune—the altars will reveal. . . .
We then shall be impulsed to kneel
And send a prayer upon its way
For those who wear the thorns today.

Oh, let's build bridges everywhere
And span the gulf of challenge there!

BLACK RECRUIT

At home, I must be humble, meek,
Surrendering the other cheek;
Must be a coward over here,
And yet, a brave man—over there.

This sophistry is passing strange,
Moves quite beyond my mental range—
Since I must be a hero there,
Shall I prepare by crawling here?

Am I a faucet that you turn
To right—I'm cold—to left—I burn!
Or but a golem wound to spring
This way or that—a soulless thing!

He surely is a master-man
Who formulated such a plan.

Leanna F. Johnson

Leanna Frances Johnson, a graduate of Simmons College and
Boston University, is at present Counselor, formerly teacher,
in the Washington, D. C., Public Schools.

JOY OR SORROW

Which calls forth the Muse?—
  Joy or Sorrow?

Does Joy make us sing most brilliantly,
Flame highest, break bonds with Gladness?

The throbs of Happiness surge through our words,
And croon in the cadences of Rhyme and Rhythm.
But Sorrow searches deep for thoughts,
Tears forth blunt phrases,
Brings out what was not guessed to be in us,
Makes epigrams of our experiences,
And codifies the Despair of the Ages.

SUPREMACY

You chatter of your "white supremacy" . . . . .
Now list you here!
Have you a voice more pure, more sweet,
Than this girl ushers forth
From out thick lips?
Here in this dark brown shell—
A caricature of your comic page—
From this crude mask
Come lovely notes,
So soft and unafraid.

And can the tapering fingers of your snowy hands
Blend colors truer than this boy's?

He looks a dwarf—his parents had no time
To rear him straight and tall
As yours did you.
Why do you laugh and turn aside your head?
How can you toss it high in pride and scorn?

If you are then supreme,
In your art we should see
Such fine perfection
Theirs would overshadowed be.

Ruth Brownlee Johnson

Ruth Brownlee Johnson was for eight years secretary to the
President of Wiley College, Marshall, Texas. Upon her
marriage, she resigned, and now lives in Oklahoma with her
husband, recently discharged from the Army. Her poetry has
been read over national radio stations, and has appeared in
anthologies. She is the author of *Life, Lore, Love,* a pamphlet
of poems.

C O R D S

I'm bound,
Bound with a thousand cords—
Never to be free.

Cords of the mind, heart,
Cords of power, cords of blood.
Cords of strength, will, lust, lure,
Hunger, pain, heat, and cold.
Light and darkness, noise and silence,
Relatives and friends,
Cords of love.

Running, walking, jumping.
Singing, talking, laughing.

Smiling, sighing,
Working and worrying,
Imagination, hallucination,
Sleeping and dreaming.

Cords, cords, cords—
Tightened for life,
Loosed for death,
Here or beyond I can never be free.

I'm bound,
Bound, I tell you,
Bound to a life on earth and beyond—
By cords,
A thousand cords,
A million cords,
Cords, cords, cords!

CHAINED

Memory, let me go.
Don't forever chain me to this past
That makes my heart ache so.
Soothe my tired brow;
Ease my intense pain;
Quench this bitter thirst,
Heal my ghastly scars;
Feed my hungry lips with love,

For I have a soul that has been crushed.
Memory, if you can't do this,
Then loose this chain
And let me go.

Georgia Holloway Jones

Georgia Holloway Jones has worked as assistant librarian at Prairie View College and Morgan State College, and Librarian at Camp Lee, Va. While a student of Library Science at Fisk University, she was a member of James Weldon Johnson's first creative literature class.

ENCHANTMENT

It was on the top of a hill beneath
The glittering stars that I saw you—
A hill shaped like the vaulted sky
Of heaven, and all strange and new.
From below was heard the gentle ripple
Of a flowing stream, and O, how I
Was enchanted by its distant song—
And by you, and the stars, and the sky.
How I long to catch the spirit
Of that night, and hold it fast, then draw
Upon my canvas, eternal and divine,
That moment so filled with love and awe!

TO JAMES WELDON JOHNSON

O Bard, undaunted by creed and race,
Thy spirit shall never cease
To lead us on, to set the pace
Toward right, toward peace
And victory.

And in our search for freedom's songs
Thy words will ever ring
Above the crowd, above the throngs
For us who seek and sing
For liberty.

Ed Lee

Ritten Edward Lee III served in the Air Corps during World War II, and is now a college freshman in Indiana. He has been writing poetry and singing in choirs. Except in his school paper, he has never published before.

BLEND

Black, brown, yellow, red, and white:
Mix them together . . . that's right.
They were poured in the pot;
What have we got?
America!

FREEDOM'S SNARE

Your soul isn't happy
And your conscience isn't free,
As long as you play "God"
And keep the chains on me.

MAN

Man is born to stay but a little while.
And each day he dies . . .
Passing from the scenes of this crazy world
Into endless eternities . . .

Each day . . .
Time comes violently with ugly arms
That are eager to kill
Something that lives and breathes . . .
. . . Like man!
But man rushes on unhesitatingly,

Thinking that the world is his own
. . . Thinking that God made it just for him!
And if he could
He would not be unlike a selfish child
With a toy . . .
He'd take the world in his little arms, and say,
"This is mine."

But one day
He, too, is going to be cut down,
And, like a wilting dandelion
In a torrid sun, die!

TRAGEDY

I hooked my hopes
On a shooting star,
Wishing that it
Would carry me far . . .

But my star was among the ones
That fell . . .
. . . in Alabama.

SOUTHERN JUSTICE

For I have been bitten by more than
A viper's fang. . . . .
My soul has died again and again.
Hung in trees.
Lashed . . . and lashed some more.
From somewhere blows a wind,
A wind of malice . . .
Evil eyes, with raving hatred.
Dragging me through ballast.

Blood stained ropes.
Lynch . . . lynch. . . .
And lynch some more.
Justice?
My fate is decided
Before the court convenes.
Jury?
They are prejudiced;
Even to them "it seems"
"Ten years' time, boy";
Injustice . . . . and
More injustice.

Dio Lewis

Dio Lewis attended schools in Maryland and Washington,
D. C., and lives in Arlington, Va. His work has appeared in
several magazines and newspapers.

THE MALCONTENTS

Mysterious are the ways
Of Jehovah and of mouse;
Both move upon a tip-toe
To haunt a trusting house.

One gnaws upon the tin
And finds a sturdy frame;
The other, locked from out the heart,
Steals inward just the same.

Man, Low Executioner,
Seeks a place above
The murdered who espied his trap
Of brutal cheese—or love.

TIME

He was free,
The patriarch of our house!
Stalked up and down the cellar stair,
Then garretward his course;
Rebel against the father—?
Someone did!
Caught him in a trap of springs,
(Jewel movements were the lure)
Set him in a tiny box. . . .
And blandly labelled "Swiss!"

Luther George Luper, Jr.

Luther George Luper, Jr., plays the piano with a popular orchestra in Los Angeles. During the war he worked in a California copper tubing plant as a laboratory technician. He holds a Bachelor of Science Degree from Prairie View, Texas State College, and hopes to publish a book of his poetry soon.

SONNET SPIRITUAL

A song was born amid the cotton blossoms
First throated by the vocal chords of blacks
Among the ever hunted squirrels and 'possums,
And well within the range of lashed backs.
Mingled with remorseful tears and suffering,
Seasoned with experience and emotion,
Offered to the Lord, a black man's offering,
Praise through song undying love, devotion.
Angels then bent low from Heaven's portals,
Turned their ears to hear this untrained choir;
Never had since time begun that mortals
So set the hearts of Heaven's host afire;
The song poured forth emotion, pent up love,
And reached through space to God who reigns above.

Martha E. Lyons

Martha E. Lyons, nineteen years old, is employed by the U. S. Air Forces at Wright Field, Dayton, Ohio. She hopes to enter college in the near future, and study Creative Writing.

A THING BORN OF DARKNESS

My heart is incased in rubies of red that are
Full of the seeds of malice to man, and never
Shall be dead for they—they are scarlet beads
Of glass that feed my starved mind, my brain,
My pulsing disease-filled heart.

My thoughts are bound by an oven of steel that lets
No love escape its walls, that sears the souls of
Those who heed the beckonings of my feverish call;
That makes me stomp my weaker brother and Hate!
And Hate! and Hate!

The daylight strips the naked hates that shiver
Deep within my soul, my muscles, each single
Molecule—and people take heed and they whisper
About the fruits of sin, of lies, of blind injustice.

But as the rays of truth and light curl up and go
To sleep, I keep a jealous eye on the night stealing
Over the hill, and heave a sigh of assurance for
Now I can spread evil and hate in peace, in seclusion,
In darkness!

Gertrude Parthenia McBrown

Gertrude Parthenia McBrown, a graduate of Emerson College of Drama, Boston, Mass., studied in Paris at the Conservatoire National de Music et d'Art Dramatique, and at the Institute Britannique of the Sorbonne. She was an artist pupil of the English Actress, Stella Patrick Campbell of the London Royal Academy of Dramatic Art. While in London she did research in African Folk-lore, and has dramatized several African stories. She is the author of *The Picture Poetry Book,* and is well known as a dramatic artist. Her poetry has appeared in both national and international publications.

LILACS

Come, let's walk where the lilacs grow.
Hand in hand together we will go;
And in the perfumed silence we shall know
The miracle of scented boughs when lilacs blow.

BRONZE QUEEN

God fashioned you an autumn birch
Standing stately on a hill,
Swaying in your silver gown,
Lifting high your golden crown.

God fashioned you of royal birth
Sitting on a Pharoah's throne,
Bidding men look up and live
While your smiles you sweetly give.

God fashioned you a tall bronze queen
Living nobly and serene.

Fleetwood M. McCoy, Jr.

Fleetwood M. McCoy, Jr., is a law student at the University of Michigan. He served in the Navy during World War II, "survived the destruction of two ships, and was discharged with a disability incurred during service with the Atlantic Fleet."

UNDERWAY

You drop the cold, wet tugboat's lines,
For they've finished with their work.
And your whistles blast
As the towers glide past
While you're conned for shoals that lurk;
Then you feel the surge of a long ground swell,
As you watch the shore that you love so well
Drift astern, with its blinking signs.

And a sharp, cold spray fills your face with salt;
And you're miserable, but it's no one's fault;
So you face the sea with a half-brave grin
And you curse your fear, and you call it sin.
But a thought of home makes you cry inside,
Makes you swallow all of your penny pride,
Makes you turn back the hours—to a fireside.

Then you try to call up a smile that died
When you first set foot on this joy and pride
Of the fleet. But it lies with the weight of lead
In your barren heart—for it's lying dead.
It died in the hearts of a thousand men.
For some, landfalls brought it back again—
But you think again of the countless more
Lying mute in the voice of the ocean's roar. . . .

Eldon George McLean

Born in Port-of-Spain, Trinidad, B. W. I., Mr. McLean became an American citizen while serving in the U.S. Armed Forces during World War II. Some of his poetry has been used by a Verse Speaking Choir touring New England. He is collecting a book of his poems.

GUTTER RATS

You pushed me down the gutter;
You stepped on my hands as I climbed
Every beastly rung of the ladder
To better myself and my kind . . .
But I laughed loud.
You crushed harder.
Again and again I laughed,
Louder, yet louder.
For I knew to keep me in that gutter,
You'd have to be in it, too.

BITTERNESS

The unsavory tastes of life
Sometimes make me speak with hate,
And think with the unfair scales of vengeance.
Sometimes it shakes my world of faith
And cuts ambition's lofty course with its knife.
Sometimes it ruffles my serene stream of mind
And wedges it in culs-de-sac of futile strife.
I have felt its scorching breath upon my face.
My burning heart subdued, scarred beyond repair.
And learn too late its bitterness at work,
Corroding mind with fear,
Corroding heart with hate,
And seizing my soul with pernicious prayer.

EXPERIENCE

When you have seen the ditches and the skies,
And felt your heart crumble at your feet,
You haven't only lived—
But died.
When you have tasted the pains of bloody war,
And still see the ugly hates of life triumphant,
You haven't only aged ten score,
But you have died—
Ten times more.

THE INEVITABLE ROAD

Free me from the memories of the shackle.
That's all I ask—
A simple, human thing.
You once possessed the cruel chains
That made me yours
Against God's will.
And though you have relinquished them,
You keep me in its sordid shadow.
Mark you, still against God's will.
You made yourself smaller than I
Whom you chained and called your own.
Now it seems inevitable that we must grow,
You and I, both of us together.
But the true test of growth
Depends on me to bury the hate that you deserve;
And depends on you to let this shameful shadow die.

RETROSPECTION

My heart is barren as the burnt sands of the desert.
But this heart, though barren now,

Was born of a fertile womb,
And like a beautiful flower once bloomed.
My love, though sparkling like wine,
Can never be bottled.
It's the vintage of a vandal mind.
My soul—the lucky wretch—
Escaped the agony of this prison stretch,
Fleeing on the wings of song,
Flirting with God as it left this gory ground.

Clifford L. Miller

Clifford L. Miller, writer, lecturer, and minister, is a graduate of Fisk University and Andrew-Newton Seminary. President of the Quill Club of Boston, radio speaker on "Your Brother's Voice," a race relations program, he is author of *Haunting Voice,* a book of verse, and columnist of the Boston *Guardian.*

SPRINGTIME

An old, old world
Clad in a new, new dress.
O chief Dressmaker of them all
How deft Thy fingers,
How perfect Thy workmanship,
How new yet ever old Thy patterns!

William Lorenzo Morrison

William Lorenzo Morrison, a graduate of Bluefield (W. Va.) College, lives in Washington, D. C. A malady which has afflicted him since childhood has caused him to be a shut-in. He is the author of *Dark Rhapsody*, issued by Henry Harrison, Poetry Publisher.

ETERNAL DESIRE

You have known what love can be:
Some joy, some tears and misery;
And yet I wonder if in future years
Futility may not make you long for me—
If God made desire for love that's pure
Deep in woman as eternity.

Constance Nichols

Constance Curtis Nichols runs an accounting business in Columbus, Ohio. Her short stories and poetry have appeared in several magazines. She wrote and produced a three-act play in Columbus.

CIVIL SERVICE

My desk sits facing yours across the floor,
Yet your fair head is stiffly held aloof
From my own darker one, though 'neath our roof
With one accord we do a job. For war
Has linked us as no pleading could before.
Yet, seemingly, you wait for further proof
That we are spun the same ... the warp and woof
Of human fabric, draped at freedom's door. ...
For you are still reluctant to obey
The impulse that would bring you to my side;

You send your memos on a metal tray
And coldly kill each overture I've tried.
Why hope to rid charred continents of gloom
Till we have learned to smile across a room?

BABY HAIR

I took a peek for the very first time
At the tiny brown mite on the bed.
He blinked his eyes and doubled plump fists,
And I ran to his mother and said,
"The most cunning baby I ever did see!"
But she, patiently lying there,
Touched my arm and with anxious voice
Whispered, "Does he have good hair?"

DESIRE

An artist looked up from his painting
And saw in his doorway there
A tiny maid with pecan-colored skin
And a mass of black, tangled hair!

The little lass smiled, oh so sweetly,
And said in a voice so low,
"I pass by your shop on my way to school;
You paint pretty pictures, I know.

"I wanted to ask you to paint me
With color you have to spare,
And make me white like the girls in my class
Who are all so lovely and fair."

The artist stared down at the youngster
And said, "Oh, you silly mite.

Do you think if I change that skin of yours
It will make everything all right?

"Do you think that mother would know you,
Or Daddy would hold you tight?
Do you think they would let you by the door
If your skin were all painted white?

"Don't think white skin is better than brown!
Each hue's from the same, sure hand
That brushed all the blue up into the sky,
That spattered the green on the land!

"So be on your way, my little lass.
Stay there in your own wee place!
Be happy to know God's one wish of you
Is a smile on that dear brown face!"

Rev. John Henry Owens

Rev. Owens has held various government jobs, both in Washington and California, and pioneered on a ranch in California. His poetry has appeared in several anthologies and about twenty magazines, here and abroad.

THE ANSWER

The day brought confusion and night brought
despair,
So I whispered my story to God in a prayer;
My strength was too feeble, my courage seemed
gone,
But God sent new courage on wings of the dawn.

THE ALTERNATIVE

If I use scorn when love would be more kind,
Then carelessly I loose the ties that bind—
To man below and to our God above,
And shuts me from His tender breath of love.
If I should scorn one of God's human race,
Upon what premise shall I beg His grace?

Gladys Marie Parker

Gladys Marie Parker has written short stories for various
publications; she does water colors, pen sketches, oils and clay
modeling. One of her landscapes on exhibit at Howard University won honorable mention. She prefers doing portraits,
and designing. She is now a regular columnist for the Washington, D. C. edition of The Pittsburgh *Courier*.

THE DREAM

Once upon a dreary evening
In the midst of the world's despair,
I stumbled into a lovely dream
And found you waiting there.

The gloom and the sorrow faded
As fog in the sun's golden ray,
And the hour for which I had waited
Like a treasure had come my way.

From the moment I first saw you—
Sweet and lovely and so demure—
Hopes and dreams I have built around you
Of a love so deep and sure.

And now in the placid hours
Which the wonders of love unfold,
To these dreams I have added others
Of days rich in joys untold.

So come where the stars are shining,
And the moon dips low from its berth.
We will follow the road that is winding
O'er the breadth of God's green earth.

We will find our nook by the wayside
Where love eternally grows,
Where faith and hope are allied
And the warmth of its goodness glows.

Out of moments of strife and sorrow
Came my vision so lovely and fair
That there need be no dream of tomorrow—
Love shall always be waiting there.

Jesse F. Patterson

Jesse Franklin Patterson, a veteran of World War I, lives
in New York with his wife and four children. He is a ma-
chine operator.

W A R

Hope, and the love of life that's in it;
The scream of the shells, the voice of the guns,
And the deep, grim purpose that's over it all;
To kill, to cripple, and to maim;
To desecrate in the Master's Name—
And that is War.

Love, and the ache of the heart that's in it;
The curtain of dark, with its strain and its fear;
The wet, the mud, and the bed in the earth;
The oaths and the weariness that give them birth;
To kill, to cripple, and to maim;
To desecrate in the Master's Name—
And that is War.

GRILL ROOM

Dirty grey smoke wreathes dirty brown walls.
Sleek brown men with dirty souls . . .
Sweat and noise and toasts,
Dirty stories and drunken boasts.

Big black women, little yellow women—
All kinds of women with hard, hard faces.
Old women, painted, with eyes too bold,
Young women, painted, with eyes too old.

Sweating musicians with big liver lips,
Jelly-roll dancers with undulating hips.
Rot-gut gin to drive away old sorrow . . .
Jungle men tonight—white folk's boys tomorrow.

Robert N. Perry, Jr.

Robert N. Perry, Jr., is employed by the Boy Scouts of
America in New Orleans. He began writing poetry in college,
and won several prizes. Contributor to *Negro Voices,* he is
now working on a historical novel. He has arranged and com-
posed a great deal of music for use with glee clubs.

THE SEASONS

Winter is an old man,
Bent with the pain of years
That mark time,—
And gaunt with the bareness
Of blasted nakedness,
Whitened by dry-drifted snows,
Wrinkled by rain-winded cold,
And cut by drumming sleet.

Spring is a young girl,—
Risen in the early morning
From dreams of her lover,—

Offering a glowingly vibrant body,
Graceful and as perfect as the wings
Of a fleet swift,—
A moving bit of darkness
Flying at evening
Over the hushed smoothness
Of a hidden pond,—
Awakening to a new-felt but ancient urge,
Stirring and bounding,
Moving and striving
For infinite expression
In life, love, and beauty incarnate.

Summer is an answered prayer
Of a beautiful woman
Who has loved well,
And looks upon her children with joy;
Living her life again
In the life they live,
A peaceful life,
A song of exquisite tenderness
Blending the fitted harmonies
Of muted heartstrings,
Rushing down fluted columns
Supporting echoing and re-echoing domes
Of Nature's temple,
Shining in ivory whiteness of cold beauty,
Saving the best for the Master Harvest of

Autumn, death and life and fulfillment,
To a world ready for sleep,
Cutting its certain angular swath
With irregular but awful strokes
Through the field of human grain
The reckoning time of the year,
And the giver of good gifts
And fruits of the earth.

INEVITABILITY

What had you to lose?
It was then or later—
And then would have been better—

Since you fear so much now—
A moment of forgetfulness,
And an eternity of regret.

OF DICTATORS

Aye!
We have drunk
Of the wine of power
Which has robbed us
Of our senses.

Our brains work
In a tangled whirl.
Our thoughts run the gamut
Of intoxicated imagination.
But—we drink on!

We are drunken—with power;
And our tempers heat themselves
In the flaming forge of Fame.
We have become wroth—
And our angers flare.

Whom the gods would destroy
They incense and arouse
To rage uncontrollable—
And we are mocked—
Of the gods.

Lucia M. Pitts

Lucia M. Pitts came to Washington from Chicago in 1933 and, by the end of 1942, had risen from a secretary to an administrative assistant in the government in Washington to an Employee Relations Representative back in Chicago. She later saw service in the WAC during World War II, at Fort Huachuca, Arizona; Birmingham, England; and Rouen, France. She is now manager of Pitts' Personal Service. Her writings, mainly poetry and articles, have appeared in numerous anthologies, newspapers and magazines and her poetry has been read on several radio stations. She was a member of the Editorial Board of *Negro Voices*, which also published several of her poems. With Tomi Carolyn Tinsley and Helen C. Harris, she collaborated in a privately printed book of poetry called *Triad*. Her play, "Let Me Dream," was written for and performed by Co. B, 6888th CPD, WAC, in Rouen, France.

LET THEM COME TO US

Now they go forth to war,
Our white brothers across the sea,
Speaking wistfully of peace.
They have known peace;
Now they go forth to war.

We who are black,
All the days of our lives
We have known war;
All the days of our years
We have lived war.
We are not acquainted with peace;
But if our brothers would learn of war,
Let them come to us.

If they would know aggressors,
Let them come to us and hear how we, forever long,
Have been set upon by demons of hate
That spring from hearts that know us not
But attack us still.
Hear how, not for one or five years of our lives

But for eighty long years and two,
We have been made to defend ourselves
Against the unseen and the seen, within and without—
   inertia and indifference, violence and hate,
   starvation and sickness, envy and betrayal,
   ignorance and illiteracy, guns and bombs,
   misunderstanding and injustice,
   ropes and faggots . . .
Hear how these aggressors and countless more
Have invaded our homes and left them a shambles,
Robbed our hearths of fathers and sons,
Laid waste our growing fields,
Hanged our hearts on the tree . . .

If they would know of aggressors,
Let them come to us.

If they would face the foe unflinching,
If they would learn to fight unceasing,
Let them come to us and see—
See how, with unflagging hearts and heads and hands,
Out of the dust that sifted under our nomadic feet
And the blood of our fathers spilled in battle,
We have fashioned men.
See how, with too little for food,
We have made them strong—
Strong to run, strong to fight,
Strong to dig the world's ditches,
Lay its gleaming rails across the land
And push its buildings up to brush the skies.
See how, by candle-light and guttering lamps,
And by the kindly light of the moon
We have taught our men and made them wise,
So that now they walk serene and unfaltering
With men of tools and plows and figures,
Men of medicine and law and government,
Those of frocks and words and palettes,
The world of footlights and music and song . . .

Then let them look again and see
How we, grown strong and wise,
Have tramped the mountains and the plains,
The long and thickly matted swamps,
Sodden with the blood of our neighbors,
Our fathers and our brothers,
To meet the foe and face him down—
How we have faced both master and menial
In open combat and in hidden dug-out,
And snipers in the world's labyrinth passes.
We have faced unafraid the marching invader;
We have met death by cruel violence
At the hands of "persons unknown."
But in spite of the numberless wounded and dead,
We have plunged on and never turned back.

If they would know the strength to fight,
Let them come to us.

If they would have faith—
If they would keep hope forever alive,
If they would know patience akin to Job's,
Let them come to us and learn
The faith of our fathers;
Behold the hope that, dying, is reborn
And lives again to stiffen up our backs;
See with what patience we have borne
The pain and the losses of all these years.

If they would know hope and faith and patience,
Let them come to us.

If they would know victory in the end,
Our white brothers who go to war,
Let them come and walk with us
Who push forever on,
Who have fought a thousand wars
And died a thousand deaths,
Yet snatched victory from defeat.

Now they go forth to war,
Speaking wistfully of peace.
We, who are black, have known no peace,
But if our brothers would learn of war,
Let them come to us.

ONE APRIL

It's our anniversary.
I've had one drink—
Two drinks—
Three . . .

On our anniversary
I had several drinks
Alone.

NEVER, NEVER, NEVER

For ever and ever and ever,
Beyond time and space,
Never, never, never
Will peace know my face . . .

My soul has torment for its daily bread;
For calm my heart seeks out turmoil instead.
I find cave-depths for my lonely abode
And furnish my home in confusion's mode.

From my depths I beg of a distant star
A ladder of hope to climb where they are;
But the stairs they offer fade out in mid-air—
My arms will not reach to the sky from there.

I plead to the sun when day comes at last
And my struggles with distant stars are past;
But on sun-stairs I meet only flame and burn
And so to my depths, exhausted, return.

For ever and ever and ever,
Beyond time and space,
Never, never, never
Will peace know my face . . .

IF EVER YOU SHOULD WALK AWAY

If ever you should walk away from me
With set, immobile face, and close the door
On all that has been ours or yet might be,
So will the door remain, and swing no more.
Its hinges shall grow rusty with disuse,
Its boards shall crack and mould with coming age;
Yet I inviolate will keep, and muse
On things here in our book, save that last page.
The dark may come and settle 'round my room,
The close scent as of musk bear down on me;
Still will I strain within the gathering gloom—
With heavy, burning eyes, will strain to see.

Until the dark descends to lift no more,
Inviolate I'll sit, and watch the door.

AFTERNOON OFF

My poor wealth had been spent, that afternoon off,
And my purse was distressingly flat.
There was really no accounting for it, at all—
It had simply gone. Just like that.

I chided myself as I threaded my way
Down New Street, in and among the crowd.
Oh, I said quite awful things to myself;
And I *would* do better, I vowed.

But then I saw them—the flower vendors, I mean,
With blossoms of every bright hue.
And—well, five shillings went for the yellow ones.
Don't chide . . . Food for my soul was overdue.

POETS

Pity us, the poets.
Poor fools, it is ours
To sing and to dream,
Fumbling with the stars
And the sheen of the moon—
Ever fashioning words
Into flaming phrases
The world may not read—
Being afraid, no doubt,
Their star points will pierce the mind,
Their flame burn the heart . . .

William I. Powell

William I. Powell is a licensed engineer in New York and
New Jersey. He has written extensively for technical publications, and invented a new device not yet patented.

BLUE MELODY

When dusky hands through ivory keys unfold
    The thoughts to them beyond all writ or word,
And some brown girl, in chant, begins to scold
    The man she loves, by some new siren lured,

Then through the air held tense by rhythmic croon,
  Love's violent drama do I see portrayed.
This voice, bewailing of some unseen wound,
  Anguish beneath that brown skin has displayed.

Such music never is fruit of paler hands.
These notes which with my spirit would commune
Come not from written theme or score of bands,
  But are the spawn of soul and mind attuned.

Brown girl, would that the world could understand
  The boundless depth your passioned voice implies,
That harks to life in far-off tropic land,
  And in me sounds a note that never dies.

J. Farley Ragland

Dr. Ragland, a graduate in Pharmacy, is proprietor of the Campus Pharmacy in Lawrenceville, Va. He is the author of three books of poetry, the latest, *Rhymes of the Times,* published in 1947. He wrote the theme song of the National Negro Exposition in Chicago, 1940, and his poetry has appeared in several anthologies, and been broadcast.

UNCLE TOM

There he goes with his hat in his hand—
An old-time feature in a new-time land.
His poor eyes popping in a fawning grin,
He shuffles along among his fellow men.

Always looking to apologize—
Belittling the efforts of his race to rise—
Whether it's wrong or whether it's right,
Always bowing to a face that's white.

Poor Uncle Tom—he does not know
His day was over long ago!

Now is the time when we must be strong,
And take more pride in the Black Man's Song!

It matters not if we're black or tan;
It doesn't take color to make the man!
We're in the race, and sink or swim,
We'll keep our pace with the rest of them!

STRICTLY SPEAKING

Don't tell me that I'm loyal
Though my face is black or brown,
Then have a battle-royal
And shoot my people down.

Don't say I should be quiet
In fidelity and pride,
Then have a racial riot
With policemen on your side.

You praise my "Aunt Jemima"
For the service she has done—
Then a mob in Alabama
Beats and burns her only son!

We are tired of empty phrases
And of childish ballyhoo—
Stop the "Jim Crow" Dixie raises;
That's the human thing to do!

BLACK AND TAN

She was Nordic's creamy white
With classic features, clear and bright,
But in her eyes there shone a light
For the dark brown boy beside her.

Her dainty perfumed fingertips
In multitudes of tender trips
Pressed warmly to the shapely lips
Of the dark brown boy beside her.

In satisfying soothing bliss
He quaffed the nectar of her kiss;
She loved the ecstasy of this—
The dark brown boy beside her.

And though this maid of Aryan race
Possessed a queen's exotic grace,
There was devotion in her face
For the dark brown boy beside her.

East is East, and West is West,
But love is his whose love is best—
This Nordic miss found happiness
With the dark brown boy beside her.

Edward Richards

Edward Richards was born in Saint Thomas, Virgin Islands,
and his poetry was first published in the local papers while
he was attending Charlotte Amalie High School. Later his
first book of selected lyrics was printed in the Virgin Isles.
When World War II broke out, he enlisted in the U. S.
Navy, and at present he is an Officers' Steward, stationed in
Norfolk, Va. His poetry has appeared in the *Afro-American,*
the *People's Voice* and other publications.

FEAR

His guiding star
Cast our shadows
Quietly behind us.
Upward we climbed,
Hand in hand.

His dream in my heart
And my dream in his heart
Were one.
Instead of concentrating
On the star,
We kept gazing
At our shadows
Until it seemed we saw
Someone coming
To attack us.
"Let's turn back!" he stammered.
He raised an empty hand
To strike the first blow
In self-defense.
There was no attack.
He tried to run away
Down Democracy's highway
Hoping I would let him go,
Hoping he could pull me back.

Constantia E. Riley

Constantia Riley is a native Pennsylvanian whose hobby is collecting antiques. Her poetry has appeared in the Chicago *Defender* and other papers.

A D I E U

Let me steal gently from the marts of men
When the sun is sending forth her ray;
So my faint adieu is lost in the din
Of incessant toil that fills the day.

Speak to none of my departing
Till my bark is safe upon her way,
Leaving an echo upon embarking
In the form of still and worthless clay.

Etholia Arthur Robinson

Etholia A. Robinson, a native of Macon, Ga., is a social worker, at present employed by the Bibb County Welfare Department.

WHAT IS GOD?

They tell me you are a far-away God
Who acts as a recorder and a judge.
Some say you are an indulgent Father
Who sits and watches over men, and sees to all their
needs.

I try to feel and understand you
As being a God of the description given,
But all my efforts have been in vain,
For you reveal yourself to me in everything.

I stretched myself in the great expanse of nature—
You are so near to me that I feel you
As you breathe upon me in the vibration of the wind,
Sending cares and troubles away.

I listen when I hear your calm sweet voice
Chiming to me from below
And, on looking, I see your smiling face
Mirrored in a silvery stream.

When evening comes, I see you—
The noted and masterful artist—
As you skilfully and gracefully tint all nature
With beautiful and harmonious colors.

I have looked into the blue above and the green
below,
But everywhere I go I find you,
Not the far-away God nor the indulgent Father,
But the dynamic force of life.

Ruth E. J. Sarver

Ruth E. J. Sarver, in private life Mrs. Marcellus Jacobs, is a Staff Sergeant in the WAC, now stationed in California. She is the author of *Fantasies of a Lover, Fantasies,* and *Fantasies Troisieme,* and is a violinist, athlete, newspaperwoman and business executive.

THE COMPENSATION

Once I asked for one lone petal of a rose,
To scent its fragrance, feel its touch.
And since I asked so little, I suppose,
I was given more than twice as much.

Once, in dreams, I asked one hour alone with you,
To sense your nearness, view your charms
As if my every wish had fallen due,
You spent the entire dream-night in my arms.

DREAM LOVE

Blame me not for pleasing castle dreams
Built on plastic stairs ascending high
Into the realm of sated pseudo-love.

Since earth proclaims no current mate for me
To fondle or adore,
In dreams, then, let me leave this earth
And mount my mystic stairway
To the stars.

Will Smallwood

Will Smallwood has been writing for newspapers and magazines since he was fourteen. A Californian by adoption, he
spends most of his travelling time in New York where he does
radio scripts. He is the poet discovery of the late Rob Wag-
ner, of *Script* magazine fame. His poems appear frequently
in foreign publications.

COME, BELOVED

Come, take my hand, beloved, for it is midnight;
We have a rendezvous on a hillside with God.
He lives there and it will be easy to find Him.
The mantle of night will cover your hair;
Stars will serve as candle light;
I have fashioned you sandals for the meadows below;
On wings of night-wind we will hear soft singing;
The sea is a jewel afar and magnificent;
This night of our pilgrimage is beautiful;
It mirrors the serenity my soul finds in yours;
It holds heartbeats measuring our minutes together.
Hold fast my hand, beloved, we must go;
He waits there in the clover,
For I have made a promise
To come at midnight, in joyful thanksgiving,
For His gift of you to me.

I OWN A DREAM

To stand with you at close of day,
With sunset in our eyes, is to find refuge.
To gaze at the vesper star, then turn to you
With a murmur on my lips, is to know proud content.
There is naught in the world at eventide, but God
         and us—
There are no homing birds, no songs, no flowers,
For what would they be but trespassers?

To have your hand in mine is happiness unto itself;
The world is our cathedral, and love is our
                              benediction.
There is no beginning, there can be no end;
All of it is dream-like with awakening not to be
                              feared,
For it is a dream which I shall always own.

PLEDGE

Let us promise ourselves this:
When this interlude grows stagnant,
We will release it, as a swift bird,
Bidding it Godspeed and safe flight
Onto other high-flung branches.

FORGIVENESS

While I search your face for forgiveness
Your tears are transparent pearls
Mirrored in my eyes as raindrops
On wet bronze.

James Edgar Smith

James Edgar Smith, a graduate of the Atlanta University
School of Social Work, served for three years in the U. S.
Marine Corps, and is Program Director of the Phyllis Wheat-
ley Community Center in Greenville, S. C.

FRAGILITY

I crushed a little flower,
A rose it was, I know,

For even at this hour
My fingertips smart and glow.

A rose is a fragile thing . . .
But I had no way to tell
What sadness dead flowers bring
Till the petals fell.

SHADOWS

Shadows of trees at night
Draw pictures on the ground
That cling to the earth so tight
They cannot make a sound.

They lie in quiet repose
With dew upon their cheek,
And only the moonlight knows
Why shadows are so meek.

Jules Wynn Smith

Jules Wynn Smith is preparing for a concert career as a
baritone. His talents and experience in the fields of music
and the theater paved the way for his work in many Hollywood screen productions.

A QUOI BON?

A joyous nymph with childlike pride
takes wings and flitters near my side
and whispers in sardonic glee
that all who love should thus feel free
to sip the nectar from the flower
which hangs unblushed from yonder bough.

Of what avail?—should I caress
that which I shall always possess?
To pluck and breathe its perfumed breath
my fairest flower would swoon in death.
I am content that I should see
each bud in all its ecstasy
send forth its fragrance through the air—
the symbol of an earthly prayer.

So tempt me not with mystic powers;
I am the keeper of the flowers.

Theodore Stanford

Theodore Stanford is City Editor of the Pittsburgh Edition
of the Pittsburgh *Courier,* and former World War II war
correspondent for that paper, covering activities of Negro
troops in Europe, Asia and North Africa. In 1946 he was
awarded a citation by Secretary of War Patterson for his
work as a combat correspondent. The Bureau of Negro Affairs, Philadelphia, published a volume of his poetry in 1936,
under the title of *Dark Harvest.*

THAT VENGEANCE GATHERS

I have in anguish sought to comprehend
The deep persistent folly of the rich
Man's way; the inexorable and vain
Illusions of his lust; and I have seen
The treacherous foundations upon which
The tottering dimensions of his strength
Are built: greed, fear, oppression, pale deceit.

But from the gouged and prostrate bodies of
His captive towns—that skyward thrust
Stone breasts which hold unheeded portent of
New pyramids—I have remarked the sounds
That vengeance gathers in its issuing.

—132

Norman Hills Stateman

Norman Hills Stateman started writing poetry while attending elementary school in Metuchen, New Jersey. At present he is working as Associate Editor of a newspaper, the *People's Chronicle*.

AREN'T WE ALL?

I'm proud of this brown skin of mine,
Broad nose and curly hair;
I'm glad it's there.
I'm proud of the way I walk and talk
And sing and pray,
And am thankful that I can do my share
Of work each day.
I'm proud of the blood that fills my veins;
It's pure and whole,
And I'm proud of the God I worship
Within my soul.

Oh, yes—
And people of my race, I'm proud of you,
And you're proud, too.
We're all proud.
It's no disgrace to be a member
Of minority's few.
I think they envy you.

Keep you down? They can't
No matter how they try.
Have not you heard them cry
"Keep him back! His face is black"?
Let them try it, if they will.
Your genius' mind and expert's skill
Will lead you on and on
Until your chance arrives.
A chance is all you need—
That chance will come in time, indeed,
And well-earned peace will fill your lives.

Oh, yes—
I'm proud of my great history.
From bond and chain I came,
But not in shame!
I'm proud of the journeys we have made
And of the fighting we have done
And still must do in time to come,
And you can see I'm happy as can be
That God made me just what I am—
A Colored Man!
So very glad am I that I could cry
Or shout out loud
To let the whole world know
I'm proud.

Isabelle McClellan Taylor

Mrs. Taylor writes poetry regularly for her hometown newspaper, and her work appears in the Pittsburgh *Courier*, and others. She is preparing a book of her verse.

LOVING BEAUTY IS LOVING GOD

He did not know that loving beauty is loving God,
But he admired an evening sky in Winter,
Mauve and silver in the fading sunset,
And snow like diamonds falling in the night.

He felt expectancy at Spring's approach, with trees
in leaf,
And the golden glow of daffodils and silver pussy-
willows.
How he enjoyed the fragrance of the lilacs,
And the sweet, white clover!

And he exclaimed in June at sapphire skies
With floating clouds like flocks of far-off sheep,
Was comforted in fields of new grown grass
That smelled of earth and rain and dew and sun.

He was delighted with the petals of the rose,
Passing in the wind at start of Summer,
And children merrily defying heat in parks and pools,
Running, carefree, with clothes a-tatter and bare
                            brown feet.

He was transfixed in Autumn, when the leaves, now
                            gold,
Float gently down and form a myriad carpet on the
                            ground
To shield the tender roots of things from Winter
                            snow.
He did not know that loving all His beauty is loving
                            Him also.

THE LYNCHING

The moon lights the wooded death spot
To the shame of the wide-spreading tree;
The leaves wail in rustling protest
Their whispered threnody.

A cloud veils the moon into darkness;
The stars shine less brilliantly;
And the voice of the dying black man
Cries, "Hast Thou, too, forsaken me?"

See how the battered body falls
In a heap when they cut it down!
See how the red, red blood flows
From the black man on the ground!

PEACE AND PRINCIPLE

It is not "peace at any price" to which the world now
must aspire,
Overlooking evil underlying motives and the desire
To leave a loophole, where in some future time,
The sword shall thrust again its bloody edge.

There has been enough of blood, wasted by the
nation's youth,
For now and for all time to come.
Enough of cities laid to waste in war's destruction,
Of faith lost in the face of fear, brutality, and
starvation!

Not peace alone must be the ultimate goal,
But liberty in a liberal thinking world.
Herein alone lies the hope of future peace:
When men shall live and let live, then shall wars cease.

Strive then for peace with principle hard set,
And faith to strengthen amity misused.
No compromise with wrong can right the cause,
But smolders slowly in a future consequence.

IN SOME TIME HENCE

In sometime hence, in some well-doing year
When we have done with war,
And all have learned the consequence of fear,
And needless waste of blood and life,
And things that man has worked long to achieve;

In sometime hence, I pray, O God,
That history not repeat itself,
Inflicting sorrow, heartbreak, and destruction,
Tearing down the very bulwark of civilization
Which we endeavor to pass on to our posterity.

Now, and in this future time,
This time of reconstruction
Of all that greed and hate has torn apart,
This picking up of pieces here and there
In every corner of this near-to-crumbling world;

Give us of faith again, I pray,
And let our trust in Thee
Be ever in our troubled thoughts,
That we regain the dignity our souls have lost
In power and greed and hate and wasted blood.

D. Gatewood Thomas

David Gatewood Thomas is organizer and President of the
State Federation of Male Glee Clubs in Virginia, and Busi-
ness Manager of the Philharmonic Glee Club of Norfolk,
Va., his home town. His poetry has appeared in many national
newspapers and magazines. His book, *The Voice from the
Wilderness*, being prepared for publication.

I THINK I THOUGHT A LIE

There was a time when I was young
In body and in mind,
I formed conceptions all my own
Of many different kind;
But now that I am more matured
It stands to reason why
That when I think of what I thought,
I think I thought a lie.

I then believed in Santa Claus
And all that people said;
I thought he came down the chimney
As I lay in bed;
And if I happened to be bad

That boogie man was nigh,
But when I think of what I thought,
I think I thought a lie.

Now when I asked just where I was
Before my natural birth,
They told me I lived up above
And came down to the earth;
My means of transit was a stork
Who brought me through the sky,
But when I think of what I thought,
I think I thought a lie.

They taught me blessed are the meek,
And that I should obey
The doctrine of the golden rule
In all I do and say;
I thought such was the proper course
And so sought to comply,
But seeing what it's done for me,
I think I thought a lie.

I always heard that married life
Was one of constant bliss,
A state that every honest man
Should labor not to miss,
So with that idea in my mind
I gave the same a try,
But as I think of what I thought,
I think I'll pass that by.

I used to think that ministers
Were truly men of God
And that their every little act
Was in divine accord;
Now that this fancy can be true
I would not dare deny,
But when I think of some I know,
I think I thought a lie.

King Solomon said in speaking of
The goodness of a name
That it in value far excelled
What riches we might claim;
I thought he was the wisest man
But when I go to buy,
If I have nothing but a name
I'll find I thought a lie.

We've all heard men of fading years
Boast of themselves and say:
That in the things they used to do
They're just as good today,
That Father Time has favored them
And they are just as spry,
But when I think of what they thought,
I think they thought a lie.

The histories I've read point out
In eighteen sixty-three
That Mr. Lincoln by his act
Proclaimed the Negro free,
But these discriminating bonds
Which still our manhood tie
Makes me in thinking what he thought
To think he thought a lie.

They told me when the cries of war
Impaired our destiny,
That fighting for the Stars and Stripes
Would save democracy;
In haste I gathered up my arms
And went to do or die,
But when I think of what I thought,
I think I thought a lie.

Our Constitution plainly reads
That color, creed or race
Shall never prove a barrier

Nor equal rights efface,
And so I thought all citizens
Could on the same rely,
But when I think of what I thought,
I think I thought a lie.

And so within the scheme of life
The things of which we dream
We find in time are things apart
And not just what they seem;
The fallacies of youth as formed
Truth will in time decry,
And so in thinking what I thought
I KNOW I thought a lie.

Tomi Carolyn Tinsley

Tomi Carolyn Tinsley, a graduate of Virginia State College, attended Chicago Park Institute, and did free lance writing in that city for a number of years. Now a professor at the North Carolina College in Durham, she has been widely published in magazines and newspapers, and has co-authored a volume entitled *Triad* with Lucia M. Pitts and Helen C. Harris.

I AM MAN

I am man.
I belong to the class mammalia,
To the species homo sapiens.
I am a descendant of the oldest fossil primate, Java.

I am human.
Red blood pulses hot in my veins.
I dream, hope, aspire;
I know the joys of laughter,
The pain of tears, dissolution, disappointment,
The devastation of hate.

I am a Negro—
Black, brown, yellow.
I've heard the rumble of tom-toms in darkest Africa,
I've sung my songs outside my cabin door,
And I've carried them to Carnegie Hall.
I know all about hell's civilization.
I ought to know;
I am a part of it.

And because I am man—
Human, vibrant,
I shall live.
Through my press I will educate;
In my schools I will teach;
And the white man will be liberated—
His soul set free as my poor body was
When Lincoln freed the slaves.
Then I shall sing my songs wherever I please—
The White House shall be my home if I choose!
And I shall live—Lord, how I shall live!
For I am human—
I am man!

CYNIC

In some distant year,
should you come to me
sans lovers,
sans unrest, uncertainty—
sans everything
save love in your beautiful
eyes for me,
I'd reach for my halo,
try on my wings.
For only in heaven could happen
Such a miraculous thing!

CLASSIFIED AD

One heart for rent;
Young—but a bit battered and bent.
Perhaps with love and gentle care,
It'll become as new—fit to wear.

There's a crack in the middle—
But it's healing, too.
For rent one heart. Who will?
Will you?

RETALIATION

You said you're crying,
I said you're lying;
You said you're through,
I said me too.
You said your heart's aching,
I said mine's breaking;
You said let's try;
I said:
Why?

Nannie M. Travis

Nannie M. Travis, a graduate of Howard University, with
an M.A. degree from Columbia University, is a teacher of
English in the State Teachers College at Fayetteville, N. C.

DARK HANDS

Dark hands, grown strong from battling with
                                    oppression,
Patient from years of unrequited toil,

Look to your skills; improve your craftsmanship;
 Hold fast to honesty.

The troubled world is racked and torn today
By brutal, grasping hands, so disciplined
In ways of treachery and lawlessness
 They seek no other course.

When this destruction shall have spent itself,
There'll be a need of clean, strong, patient hands
To cull the broken parts and build again.
 Dark hands, keep clean; prepare.

WHITE FEAR

But ever there stands through the ages
 Of humanity's ebb and flow
The immutable Law of the Harvest:
 Ye shall reap that which ye sow.

It stares through the eyeless sockets
 Of a million black men's ghosts,
And white fear rides the white man's soul
 In spite of his vaunting boasts;

For boasts and quibblings and racial myths
 And crafty maneuverings
May fool their authors a while, but a ghost
 Is concerned with weightier things.

He seeks redress for his ancient wrongs,
 Surcease of his children's pain.
How can he rest till their thwarted lives
 Are happy and free again?

Still stands the Law of the Harvest,
 Unaltered and unabeyed;
And fear will ride the white man's soul
 Till the black man's ghost is laid.

C. V. Troup

Cornelius V. Troup, President of the Fort Valley (Ga.) State College and holder of the Doctor of Philosophy degree from Ohio State University, made his first appearance in the anthology, *Negro Voices*. He has appeared in others since then.

TRAFFIC SIGNS

I wonder if, at the last day, when departed saints
    shall rise
And start their heavenly journey toward the celestial
    skies,
They will meet, as they travel upward, directing signs
    like these:
"Whites to the right, and blacks to the left, no mixing
    if you please.

"The whites may go straight to Saint Peter who
    guards the golden gate;
Just go right ahead with assurance that none will
    have to wait.
But blacks, to avoid any trouble, must detour to the
    rear,
And wait patiently till they're told to enter the city
    fair."

If such is the case in the world to come when this life
    is o'er,
Won't be hard for me, for I've learned to enter by
    the rear door.
No trouble staying to the left, it will be easy for me
For I've had *plenty* training in the blessed "land of
    the free."

Nathaniel I. Twitt

Nathaniel I. Twitt comes from the Smoky Mountain Region.
This is the first of his work to be published.

DREAM ABOUT ME

Dream about me.
Call me darling.
Whisper loving words, my dear,
How you always will adore me.
That is what I want to hear.
Breathe the thought
That naught can part us,
And forever you'll be true.
Then remember, oh, my darling,
My heart and thoughts are all for you.

Make your plans
So they'll include me
In your life from this day on.
I could never be content
If your love was past and gone.
Life grows sweeter
When the living
Is with one who holds you dear,
And your love shall be my fortress
Even when cold death is near.

If you should leave
This world before me
For a mansion in the sky,
Tell the keeper of the portal
To wait; my soul will soon be nigh.
Go, not too far, into Heaven
Where the loved ones part no more.
Wait, my darling, wait for me
Just inside of Heaven's door.

Countess W. Twitty

Countess W. Twitty is sixteen, and a sophomore at Dillard
University. She has never published before.

DEFEAT

I cannot fight a memory:
Memory, with all its shining glory
And bright beckoning ways,
Teasing you from reality
Into reverie of the past.
Memory, without the tears and pain of now.
With only the drifting flow of then.
The bright ribbon of memory
Blinding your eyes
So that you cannot see
The small threads of today
Weaving into colored ribbon of future brightness.
Turn to me . . . turn only once.
Today I can make you happy.
Tomorrow I can plan for.
But yesterday, of which I was not a part—
I can do nothing with that.
I cannot fight a memory.

HIGH TIDE

I like things that are intense.
I want my joys full, if not lasting.
No pastels will do for me
But the deep, rich color
That stands out even when faded,
So that all the world may know
That this thing, when it was new,
Was wholly satisfying,
Even if it did not last so very long.

UNREPENTANT

Because of you
I have lost my right to heaven
If heaven there be.
They tell me
There is no sin so scarlet
That it cannot be forgiven
And the soul go free
If one humbly asks.
But this sin is precious to me.
I can never receive absolution
Because I can never repent.

SUBTERFUGE

... And so we talk.
Bright empty words that mean and say nothing.
Words that are only to bridge the deep silence
That is there.
Words that are used to stop the tide of emotion that
                              would come
With overwhelming suddenness
In the quiet.
Words.
What good will they do?
They may stop the tide now,
But if it is not let out,
Bit by bit,
What will happen
When we can no longer talk,
Can no longer fool even ourselves—
Who were the last to know?
What will words do
Against the dammed up tide—
Against the flood?—

DUSK THOUGHTS

All that I can see of you
Are your swift-strong hands
Resting lightly on the porch railing.
How odd to see them so still
That ever move so surely and restlessly.
The crickets chirp in the tall oak tree
That my great-grandfather planted,
And the frogs croak in the grass at the roots of it.
The fireflies wink on and off
Like little neon lights
In the empty field just across the road.
A train rushes past a crossing
Moaning—long and sad.
But your hands do not move.
They are yet still . . . so still.

DALI FANTASY

Yellow, sickly yellow
Is the day's light
That drips over the still
And splashes on the floor.
One puddle of light
Settles there and draws me to it.
Out of the grey darkness I move
And stand in the ghastly yellow
Of the waning sun
That slowly slides over the rim of the earth.
The light stops drip . . . drip . . . dripping
On the floor,
Leaving only grey,
Enveloping . . . pressing . . . smothering me.

QUO VADIS

Time is swift
And the days step upon one another's heels
But still I wait within the formless void of my own
thoughts,
Suspended—still—unliving.
Others rush down the pathways of life
But I am afraid to go alone.
A guide must show me the way,
The path to take—the reason for going.
Lead me gently
Lest stumbling I fall—turn back.
Give me your leadership and your love
And I will give my unwavering trust
And blindly follow.

Naomi Evans Vaughn

Naomi Evans Vaughn lives in Columbus, Ohio. Her poetry
has appeared in *Negro Voices, American Women Poets,
Poetry Digest,* and many newspapers. Her hobby is song
writing.

MISTAKES

Ofttimes I go
Into the cupboard of my mind
And find upon its shelf
A bowl of mistakes.
I taste them and eat them
One by one
(With a side dish of regret).

BARRED

After the illness and fever had fled,
And you lay as cold as stone on your bed,
I tried to rouse you with grief and a shout—
But death had come, quietly locking me out.

Lloyd Warren

Lloyd Warren, a victim of tuberculosis since babyhood, has
spent half of his life in hospitals. In 1935, he played in "Green
Pastures," then on Broadway; later in "American Jubilee"
at the New York World's Fair, and "Native Son," both on
Broadway and on tour, until he was forced to leave the show
and return to the hospital where he spent another five years.
He hopes a new spinal operation will help him to walk without braces.

LEVITICUS TATE

Leviticus Tate is an object of hate
To the race out of which he has sprung,
For he whines and he apes
And he bows and he scrapes
To the people who treat him as dung.

He will act on the screen, and his whole race demean
Just for money and personal fame,
He will furnish a joke
For bigoted folk
Who use him to bolster their claim.

You may make plenty cash, but you're still merely
                              trash,
And a strong universal disgrace!
You deserve all the hate, Leviticus Tate,
You get from all ramks of your race.

Hazel L. Washington

Hazel L. Washington, a copy reader for the Afro-American newspaper, Baltimore, served for almost three years in the WAC, in this country and in Birmingham, England and Rouen, France.

MOTHER AMERICA

This is my mother, America,
To whom I give my service.
She is rich, bold, powerfully
Rolling from sea to sea,
Magnificent in pride and grandeur,
So is my mother, America.

We are the problem children,
My dark-skinned people and I.
When she looked and saw
Our faces black,
She locked strong chains around us—
Closed doors in our faces.

Grandfather slaved
To make her fields rich—
Sang to keep his reason.
Grandmother birthed from her master's lust
A fragile, yellow child—
Prayed to a far-off Jesus.
So she let them warm
By the kitchen fire;
Tossed out a crumb for their supper.
So did my mother, America.

I am the new dark daughter.
I know the songs and prayers of old.
They stick like sabers in my soul—
Crumbs do not still my hunger.

I wore the battle suit
Made by my mother, America.
My brothers died in foxholes,
Died for the rights of free men
In dark and foreign foxholes.

We are the new dark children,
My war-scarred brothers and I.
We seek a full-fledged freedom
For ourselves and mother, America,
And as we fought our foes abroad
We'll fight them in our land.

For the snakes that lurk in her bosom,
The rotten fruit on her green trees,
The stench besmirching her sweetness
Must die and live no more—

That she might be real America,
True and just America
And we, her own dark children,
Proud Americans.

A WOMAN AT WAR

I was a woman at war,
Deep in the whirlpools
And intrigues of war;
Dark like the days
That shroud my generation,
Brown like the khaki I wore.

War is hell—
Fire and smoke,
Blood, death, and starvation.
It is greed for conquest,
Lust for power,

Clamor for recognition:
An evil concoction of fiendish minds.

War is sorrow—
Tears and loneliness,
Ancient like the seas,
Wild as jungle beasts.

War is a game—
Played on the earth's checkerboard
By those who move
Out of turn
And change the natural pattern
Into chaos.

I was a woman at war,
Deep in the whirlpools
And intrigues of war;
Dark like the days
That shroud my generation,
Brown like the khaki I wore.

Carter Webster

Carter Webster, a musician interested in "Concert Boogie Woogie," became interested in poetry while in college. His background ranges from "King of Honky-Tonk pianist" to "Wartime Industrial Engineer."

CREATION

Into fog-horned Space
The Word was uttered.
Sharp bright wings of Light
Stabbed darkness in flight,
Then quickly fluttered
Into still-born Time.

CRUCIFIXION

Aqueous veils of darkness
Covered the beautiful eyes of Heaven,
Hiding the loveliness of Evening;
Pangs of death had stolen
The last spark of life
Under the faint light
From the last flickering Star—
Leaving a Shadow of Immortality
Clinging to a Cross.

LOUD JAZZ HORNS

Blow, blow, blow!
Black Boys, blow
Loud Jazz Horns!
Blasting, bounding bubbles—
Brass-bright gems—
Into the tired consciousness
Of a vigorous New World.
You . . . *Remember Hiroshima?*
America, your native land,
Is big-talk drunk with power,
Whirling centuries of science,
Reducing self-destruction
To moments from bloody years.
Blow, blow—blow!
Black Boys, blow
Still louder!!
Burst your lungs in long, loud laughs:
Help your money-sick white man
Forget his atomic fears.

Ricardo Weeks

Ricardo Weeks, born in Puerto Rico, came to the U. S. in 1925. He has contributed poetry regularly for several years to the Associated Negro Press, *Poet Lore, Opportunity, Negro Story, Color, Spotlighter, Civil Service Leader, New York Amsterdam News, The New York Age,* and Lionel Hampton's *Swing Book.* His first book of verse is *Freedom's Soldier.*

FLOTSAM

Beautiful wreck of a man,
Who are you?
From what far place
Did you come?
Your loyal voice enthralls me,
But who put that hole
In your brow?

Who tore off your right arm
And plucked out one of your eyes?
Who, and what did this to you,
Wreck of a man?

Your war-torn face
Coagulates my blood.
Your weary voice
Benumbs my brain.
But who blew off one of your legs?
My God!

What demon left you in this state?
Who knocked the stars
Down from your sky?
Who made your tomorrow
A shadowy thing,
Wreck of a man?

I DREAM A WAR

I dream a war
With the South again.
I dream a war
For Freedom's sake.

The war I dream
Is not a war of arms and men.
It is a war of Brotherhood
On Bigotry—

A war to make
The night and day people
Merge
And the minorities free
As the Stars and Stripes.

I dream a war
With the South again—
A war to bring disaster
And a haunting death
To the Foes of Liberty—

A war that will chant
Democracy
And the Rights of Man,
But most of all
I dream the war
For America's sake.

WINDOW WASHER

High above the city streets
He swings,
Poised on the ledges
Of Manhattan's mighty towers.
In the heat or cold

You can always find him,
High above the crowded noisy sections—
A bucket of water and a squeegee
Going swish, swish!
My God!
High upon the skyscrapers,
In a world of air,
Way above his earthly troubles,
Dangling on a leather thread . . .
Swinging.

FUGITIVE

The fox flees
Like a lamb before a hungry pack of wolves,
When the hunter and his dogs pursue him.
Ah, mine's indeed a portion . . .
I am the Fox!

FALLACY

The tall, muscled men
Run the world
While the small, weak men
Slave on.

The big, strong men
And the small, weak men
Are brothers.

Small, weak men . . .
Striving on the barren fields
Of the long, strong men.

Thin, sick men
And small, weak men
Dying . . .

The big, strong men
And the small, weak men
Are brothers.

Yet the tall, muscled men
Play God.

Jack Calvert Wells

Jack Calvert Wells taught school in Detroit for five years,
but gave it up to try writing. He is working on his first novel.

THEN I MET YOU

Then I met you, and
All the pent-up emotions
Of a tortured, weary soul
Burst forth in torrential flood.
All that was great within me
Responded to the harmony
Born of kindred souls
That had by chance
Been thrown together.
Yea, the deep currents
Of my being were caught
In a whirlpool of ecstasy,
Like two streams meeting
To cause a flood.
And in my dullard way
I contemplated building
A garden of infinite beauty.

Deborah Fuller Wess

Deborah Fuller Wess of Washington, D. C., has appeared before many church and civic groups to read her poetry, and her work has been published by the Afro American newspaper, *Pulse* Magazine, and the Associated Negro Press.

MY SEA OF TEARS

If I had caught the tears I cried,
Since you first broke my heart
And poured them in a valley, deep,
I know that I could start
A briny sea, where women,
Who must weep down through the years,
Could have a common place to come
To shed their bitter tears.
For men, like and unlike you,
After you are dead, my dear,
Will go on crushing women's hearts
And souls, year after year.

SERGEANT JERK

My uncle is a Sergeant in the Army now, you know,
But you'd think he was a Major, if you could see him
go
A struttin' and a prancin' up and down before his
men.
He stops to growl and grumble at the fellows now
and then.

"What's the matter with your collar and your necktie,
Private Joe?"
"Private Hank, you hold that rifle like you think it is
a hoe."

"I won't stand for droopin' shoulders; Private
            Jimmie, pick 'em up."
"Private Mack, your face is hairy as an ugly mongrel
            pup."

Then he drills his group of soldiers long as he can
            find the space.
And he shouts and scowls and cusses till he's dark
            blue in the face.
But when he comes home on furlough with Aunt
            Mattie on his hands,
You would think she was a Gen'ral 'cause he jumps
            when she commands.

He mops the floors and beats the rugs; oh boy, how
            he can work!
She never calls him "John" or "Jack"; she always
            calls him "Jerk."
But he never seems to mind it; he takes it on the chin
Until he's safely back in camp where he can crow
            ag'in.

Alexander Young

Alexander Young served with the U. S. Army Air Corps in
the Mediterranean Theater of Operations during World
War II. He is a member of the Little Theater Group of
America, and helped organize the Internationals' Club, a
writers' group. He has contributed to the *Chicago Defender,
Pitsburgh Courier, Kansas City Call, Afro-American,* and
other papers.

HEY, BOY!

A fellow said, "Hey, Boy!" so I hit him;
He did not say it because of my youthful
                    countenance,
        since I reach for autumn-tide,

But because my skin was tawny,
And my lips were full,
And because some time among my antecedents
    were the aborigines of Africa and America, alive
        in me.

I hit him, not for myself, but for those
And for all the little men, alive in me,
Upon whose primary labor the land waxed fat
    yielded her fine fruits and kaleidoscopic riches.

A fellow said, "Hey, Boy!" so I hit him,
And kicked him after he had fallen;
Still—I would not maim the mincing mongrel,
Nor smash the glow-worm,
And my foot refuses to crush the pink hyacinth.

When they led me to the little, lonely room
    with doors and windows stronger than my hands,
They asked me why I had misused this man;
They were all amazed when I replied,
    "This fellow said, 'Hey, Boy!'"

BEFORE A MONUMENT

Before a monument to one unknown
And martyred Negro soldier once I stood,
And thought of all the ills that since have grown
From that last conflict for the common good.
If he could see another war to make
The world safe for democracy and find
Oppressors rising in its early wake
To deal despondency to humankind . . .
I wonder, would this unknown soldier hold
His life ill-spent to have such evils ensue?
And would he leave his home and friends behind
To seek a rendezvous with death's dank dew?

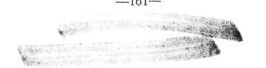

I think that he might lift his hand and cry,
"Let those who made this war go forth to die!"

LOVE'S HELPLESSNESS

I wish that you and I might have been friends
Platonically, without a show of passion,
And never known that love which oft transcends
All bounds, since ours has ended in this fashion.
But as I told you, and I still maintain,
As when at first I saw your spirit bright,
If I could meet you now all over again,
I would love you as I did on that sweet night
When moon-mist melted on your moistened face,
When low-hung weeping skies presaged our grief
And lent a strange enchantment to that place,
While our repeated kisses seemed so brief.

Yes . . . should I just now see or hear your name
Or see you once, I would love you just the same!